A Therapist Insider's Guide on Relationships

A Therapist Insider's Guide on Relationships

Healing The Past

Roxanne J. Derhodge

First Published in Canada 2014 by Influence Publishing

Book Cover Design: Marla Thompson
Typeset: Greg Salisbury
Portrait Photographer: Jon Blacker

DISCLAIMER: This book is a work of Non-Fiction. Some of the names of characters in this book may have been changed to protect their anonymity.

Library and Archives Canada Cataloguing in Publication

Derhodge, Roxanne J., 1966-, author
    A therapist insider's guide to relationships : healing
the past / Roxanne J. Derhodge.

ISBN 978-1-77141-061-8 (pbk.)

    1. Derhodge, Roxanne J., 1966- --Relations with men.
2. Man-woman relationships. 3. Interpersonal relations.
4. Mate selection. 5. Psychotherapists--Canada--Biography.
I. Title.

HQ801.D47 2014   646.7'7   C2014-904743-6

Dedicated to all the special people in my life—my parents Carol and Prince, my amazing son RJ, my lovely sister Karen and brother-in-law Ted. My nieces and nephews, Cam, Nellie, Mikes and Chants—I love to see you all together playing with RJ. Your connection takes my breath away.

You are very special, Mom and Dad. You taught me the value of family and staying connected.

Karen, my surrogate mom, you are as real as they come and have always been there for me.

RJ—as Mom always says, you are the best. I am so privileged to be on this journey of life with you. With you in my life, each and every day is a blessing.

Testimonials

"Roxanne skillfully combines personal and professional perspectives on trauma. She takes her personal story and applies her own professional expertise. She makes sense of why children who witnessed violence in their childhood family of origin are impacted in adult relationships. Her book shows others how to find their own connections between a past childhood trauma and how it affects current relationships that have gone awry. She has poignant questions at the end of each chapter to help the reader find meaning in their own childhood trauma. Roxanne's book tells us about her relentless determination to uncover why her near perfect world imploded and nearly destroyed her and how she came to understand it to move on. However, because she is a therapist she has a unique ability to critically examine theory in light of her own personal experiences. While this has allowed her to help herself it has also allowed her to help others. As a therapist I would recommend this book to anyone ready to examine their trauma history and it is also valuable for therapists who see clients with childhood experiences of trauma."

Cheryl Stock, Board Secretary, Ontario Association of Social Workers

"Roxanne has a unique way of weaving her personal story into a therapeutic process which helps us understand how our childhood experiences can shape and form who we are today. Her practical exercises at the end of each chapter enables us to identify and recognize patterns and make conscious changes to create our desired outcomes."

Laurie Flasko, CSP, Laurie Flasko & Associates Inc.

Acknowledgements

I would like to thank all the wonderful mentors that I have encountered along the way during my career path, starting with Jim Hannah, my very first clinical supervisor. Also, very important in my development was Pat Wolstenholme. Pat—you taught me the tricks of the trade when I was so very young. I was incredibly lucky to have met someone that took the time, when I was so new in the field, to show me the ropes. Also of noteworthy mention is Richard Siegel, my manager in Health and Wellness consulting. A man with a big heart, Richard took the time to let me know that he cared and helped me navigate the business realm.

My friends have been very instrumental in assisting me through the writing process. Thanks for being there for me when things did not make sense as I wrote. Your consistency and kindness gave me the strength to follow through when things got tough. Judy, Louise, Pat, Mary, Blake, Carolyn, Tam , Dan and Mo—you know how much I appreciate the last four years. The amazing women of Carsa—you have shown me kindness and caring when I needed it most in my last several years back at the Center. Thanks for your kindness and love for me and the boy.

Contents

Foreword

I first met the author some twenty years ago, when she took on the role of Team Leader of the Outpatient Department at a residential addictions treatment centre I was working at. During her time there she also became a mentor, coach, advocate and, for some of us, friend.

In her book, *How Does a Therapist Heal Their Own Relationships?*, the author offers the reader insight into key factors in the development and maintenance of relationships. She also imparts valuable information on normal human development, issues that can arise and the impact of these later in life. Using examples from her own life and healing process as a backdrop, she invites the reader to reflect on themselves and their own relationships as part of their own journey of self-discovery, learning and growth.

Roxanne Derhodge brings to her work, and this book, a mix of professionalism and warmth that the reader cannot help but find engaging.

Louise Mercier B.A.
Case Manager/Addiction Counsellor

Introduction

The Blueprint of Your Life

The life that you create for yourself, from your conception to the end of your life, is a tapestry of combined moments that are all linked together, and hopefully fit together to create your ideal life. Once you enter the world you face a vastness of possibilities, which unfortunately can sometimes become impaired by your biology or by the environment that surrounds you. When you enter this world as an infant, you are basically helpless, and in essence, your environment strongly dictates the blueprint of your life.

Not everybody's blueprint is the same. Typically, everyone begins with a different blueprint. However, a definition is needed in order to understand what a blueprint is.

Merriam-Webster's Dictionary definition states that a blueprint is:

- A photographic print in white on a bright blue ground or blue on a white ground used especially for copying maps, mechanical drawings, and architects' plans
- Something resembling a blueprint (as in serving as a model or providing guidance); especially: a detailed plan or program of action (a blueprint for victory).

The blueprint of my life has been one of fulfillment and joy all wrapped up together. My memories of my first years were filled with a lot of love and warmth, but I soon started to realize intuitively that a fair amount of pain surrounded me. As a young child, I had phenomenal dreams for my future. I would fall asleep thinking of the romance I would find and the career I would create.

For example, I always dreamed of the fairy-tale life where all the things that I desired, especially love, would be well within my reach. I looked at my surroundings through a microscopic lens and started to create the blueprint that I wanted for my life. This was the beginning of the creation of the blueprint of my life. I refused to see any of the obstacles that would block my path. Instead, I had a clear vision of what I wanted in my life and I was also definite about the things I did not want. I knew how things would look like in my life, so anything else was unacceptable to me. I developed a blueprint of my ideal life and I developed this blueprint without being fully aware of its implications. Overall, I was idealistic as I created my blueprint and did not take into account the obstacles and challenges that would eventually come into my life and force my blueprint to change.

When I reflect upon my childhood, I most often remember the good times—as most people do. My oldest sister believes that this is my greatest asset; however, I often wonder whether it is an asset or a liability. I always had big dreams, but my early childhood development also brought great pain. As I look through my family's old photo albums, I can see over time how my undeniable grin of sheer joy faded to one of hollow sadness. Even when I was younger, I unconsciously chose a path that led me to be alone in a big house with my son. Early in life I knew what I wanted, but I didn't listen to the cues around me that would have kept me on that track until it was far too late to change my blueprint.

According to Merriam-Webster's definition, many variables impacted my blueprint. These variables included biological, psychological, and social elements. I created a blueprint of my life that reveals the impact of the bio- and psychosocial elements from my inconsistent primary environment. So, what elements shaped my life? The biological elements were skewed in my favour.

My mother was physically healthy throughout her pregnancy with me. She had three healthy children and only one miscarriage before my birth. However, the environment that I was born into was less than ideal. My mother was quite young, age twenty-four, with four kids aged five and under. She was under a lot of pressure in her role as a young mother in an unstable home environment.

There was conflict within her marriage and her in-laws did not care for her because her religion was different from my father's. So, the social environment was less than ideal and my primary care environment was also filled with psychological stressors due to my parents' less than perfect marriage. Overall, environment plays a big role in your development as a child, as well as in the blueprint of your life.

I invite you to join me on the journey of my life by examining my blueprint and, in turn, to examine your own blueprint. You will not only examine the elements of my life, but you will also be able to achieve a realistic view of your own life, and to find areas for improvement. This is not to say that you have a bad life—some people have really great lives and there is not much that they need to change—instead, it might be about understanding what led you to make certain choices. In turn, these lessons can be shared with other people who can learn from them. What I want to provide here is an introspective lens so that you can discover places in your life that may need more clarity. Life is always changing, as is your blueprint. In the end, I want you to be receptive to the positive things I am going to talk about.

In Chapter 1, I outline three renowned theories that outline the stages of life: Jean Piaget's Cognitive Stages, Erik Erikson's Theory of Development, and Abraham Maslow's Hierarchy of Needs. As a reader, it is important you be aware of these various theories and see if you can understand some of the things that exist in your own life at present. The theories in Chapter 1 will be used in reference throughout the book and will help you to understand both my blueprint and your own.

At the end of each chapter, starting in Chapter 2, I include Check-In Questions, which focus on the main points in the chapter. They are also meant to challenge you to think about how these stages relate to you and your blueprint. In the end, these questions provide a way for you to both understand the chapter concepts and to relate them to your own life. In doing this, I hope to help some of you change some elements of your life. However, if you are extremely happy with your life and don't want to change a thing, maybe this information is something you may choose to share with someone who is not as fortunate and is struggling with the question of how they ended up where they are in life at this moment.

Chapter 1:
The Theories Behind Your Blueprint

The theories on the next few pages are based on Jean Piaget's Cognitive Stages, Erik Erikson's Stages of Development, and Abraham Maslow's Hierarchy of Needs and are all key to exploring the various stages of your blueprint. It is important to have a reflective lens as you work through this chapter and the rest of the book. The following three theories are instrumental in helping you understand and answer the questions posed in Chapters 4, 5, and 6 where I will walk you through the various stages and elements of my life, and then invite you to do the same type of analysis with your own life.

Piaget's theory explains how humans gradually develop knowledge, the process through which we use knowledge, and how we continue to acquire and develop knowledge. This will help you to understand the stages we go through in life from birth and ultimately, will help you develop your blueprint.

Cognitive Development Stages: Jean Piaget[1]

Sensorimotor Stage	Stage Description
Birth to two-years old	• Using body movements to learn. • Interested in things or objects around them. • If an object moves, they lost interest and move on to something else ("Out of sight out of mind.") • With time, they start to realize that things continue to exist if they do not see them; an ability termed "object permanence."

My personal reflections:

Due to the restrictions in my parents' marriage, I did not have constant freedom of movement. My mother did her best, but was quite young with four young children, so her ability to create a space where I could respond to my senses openly was limited. I suppose that I was allowed to move but it would have been limited due to my mother's time and the things that she had to manage on a daily basis, caring for the needs of four young children and an emotionally unavailable spouse.

Your personal reflections:

_____

_____

_____

_____

[1]Sources for this table include www.ehhlt.flinders.edu; www.usefulcharts.com; and www.psychology.about.com

Preoperational Stage	Stage Description
Ages two through seven	• Start to acquire language, and may use pictures to represent objects. • Thought processes developing but not yet completely logical. • Starting to realize that others can be the centre of attention rather than themselves. • Can tell past, present, and future, but still does not think in abstract terms.

My personal reflections:

My primary caregiver was under duress, so I was able to explore, but in a limited way. I started school at age three and I started to learn quite young. My exposure at school to learning was about being able to be completely egocentric. This was short-lived due to the stressors at home.

I remember that I would daydream often and would lose track of the things that were being taught in class. My little head was already full with things that I was being exposed to at home.

Your personal reflections:

_____

_____

_____

_____

_____

_____

Concrete Operational Stage	Stage Description
Ages seven to eleven	• Thought processes become more mature and adult-like. • Able to see different points of view; able to envision different scenarios of situations. • Learn that things can change, i.e. that a pile of blocks may be stacked in different ways, but there are still the same number of blocks

My personal reflections:

My academic life was enjoyable and I was quite social as a child. I did well, but at times I found it difficult to focus. Being able to have different points of view and thinking outside myself may have posed difficulties. At this point, I learned to be guarded, due to the uncertainty in my home, so I was externally focused instead of internally focused.

I found a lot of concepts difficult in math. I found it difficult to grasp and felt inadequate when I could not follow the basic principles that I needed to master in order to gain certain key foundational concepts for math. I started to tell myself that I was not good at math and science.

Your personal reflections:

_____

_____

_____

_____

_____

Formal Operational Stage	Stage Description
Age eleven onward	• Able to evaluate logic behind different situations, then make decision based on existing evidence. • Adult intelligence has been developed. • Able to think in abstract terms. • Able to think through how things may be impacted, when considering differential hypothetical information.

My personal reflections:

I was doing well in school. Even though I still had to continue to focus, due to the distractions at home, I was excelling. At twelve, I passed an exam that made it possible to attend one of the best schools in Trinidad.

Your personal reflections:

_____

_____

_____

_____

_____

_____

_____

_____

Erik Erikson's Theory of Ego Identity

Erikson's theory purports that we have a sense of who we are. In other words, our Ego Identity often changes based on daily experiences. If we feel competent, our ego motivates our behaviours and actions, and it is our ego that leads us to become competent in each and every part of our lives. If we feel mastery, then our ego strengthens. However, if our ego is managed ineffectively, then we may develop a sense of inadequacy.

Erik Erikson's Theory of Development[2]

Stage 1: Birth to age one	Stage Description
A crisis can occur when child moves from trust to mistrust. The virtue learned at this stage is **hope**.	• Learns trust based on care received from primary caregivers. • If trust is in their primary situation, child learns that, should something go wrong, there is hope for improvement. • If care is inconsistent, child starts to be guarded and mistrusting of the world, which could lead to the onset of anxiety and increased insecurity.

My personal reflections:
My parents met my basics needs. However, the issues of not trusting my environment started early; they were probably caused by the stress that I started to recognize around me. My general sense of mistrust started at that time. I would assume that I heard quarrelling and conflict, and this would be difficult for any child in this stage. If my mom and dad were embroiled in conflict, I wondered whether they would have the consistent time to meet my needs.

I think that I was probably comforted often but not each and every time that I needed soothing. So, if my comfort was inconsistent with my expectation that my needs would be met, I would have started to mistrust that I could have my needs met in a consistent way.

Your personal reflections:

_____

_____

_____

_____

_____

_____

_____

_____

_____

_____

_____

_____

[2]Sources for this table include www.psychology.about.com; www.simplypsychology.com; and www.usefulcharts.com

Stage 2: Age two to three	Stage Description
A crisis can occur when child moves from autonomy to shame and doubt. The virtue learned at this stage is **will**.	• Needs encouragement in order to explore what they can do within their limits. • Should be encouraged to do things within their limitations, but should not be criticized if they have accidents. • Needs appropriate encouragement so that shame and doubt do not develop. • If criticized, the child could become overly dependent on others and might doubt their abilities.

My personal reflections:

I went through this stage pretty well, but I remain unsure that I had undivided attention from my mom. She was under a lot of stress with four young children and not much support. My father would play with me as a child, but my mom did everything else related to my needs. I think that I would have started to want more from my parents, but when it was not forthcoming then this is when doubts about my emotions may have started.

Your personal reflections:

_____

_____

_____

_____

_____

_____

Stage 3: Age four to six	Stage 3: Age four to six
A crisis can occur when child moves from initiative to guilt. The virtue learned at this stage is **purpose**.	• Gains confidence by trying new things. • Need for encouragement is important. • If encouragement is lacking, the child may develop an inferiority complex. • Desire to try new things and succeed at them. Plan new activities and make up new games. • Desire for ongoing knowledge, but if that is not encouraged, they will feel guilty for having those needs.

My personal reflections:

I gained a bit of independence going to school, but I'm unsure that I took initiative on my own with much success. I was apt to develop guilt over needs and desires to the competing concerns that I had (home versus school).

Your personal reflections:

_____

_____

_____

_____

_____

_____

Stage 4: Age seven to twelve	Stage Description
A crisis can occur when the pre-teen moves from industry to inferiority. The virtue learned at this stage is **competence**.	• Sense of self develops when trying new things. • Desire to demonstrate a skill that is admired by others to gain approval and praise. • Peer group becomes major part of self-esteem. • May feel inferior if not encouraged to try new things.

My personal reflections:

I attained a certain amount of competence at school, but I still felt a bit uncertain of myself at times, because I felt inferior to my peers. I felt like my peers had more overall support from their parents. I went home to a high-conflict home while they went home to peaceful ones. I felt like I had to keep the dysfunction at home a secret. I felt "less than" and wished to feel at ease as I noticed the rest of my peers felt.

Your personal reflections:

_____

_____

_____

_____

_____

_____

_____

Stage 5: Age thirteen to nineteen	Stage Description
A crisis can occur when the teenager moves from identity to role confusion. The virtue learned at this stage is **fidelity**.	• Take care in how they look to others. They start contemplating "Who am I and what do I want to do when I grow up?" • Thoughts of career, relationships, family, etc. • Unable to identify who they are in society can lead to role confusion.

My personal reflections:

I was able to forge out my identity, but I was really concerned about a romantic relationship. My need to be in a relationship overshadowed other things so I was very confused. Among my peer group I was the first to marry right after university. I felt the need to have someone to love early. I needed to fill that void, which I have felt all my life, and have someone love me forever.

Your personal reflections:

_____

_____

_____

_____

_____

_____

_____

Stage 6: Age twenty to thirty-four	Stage Description
A crisis can occur when the adult moves from intimacy to isolation. The virtue learned at this stage is **love**.	• Young adults fall in love and get married. • If there is no emotional intimacy in a relationship, they may feel isolated. • Successfully manoeuvring this stage requires experiencing commitment, safety, and security through relationships.

My personal reflections:

I fell in love at quite an early age, which countered my fear of being alone, but I'm unsure that I really knew what real intimacy was at the beginning of this relationship. I thought if someone was nice to me, loved me, and would not abuse me emotionally or physically, then this was intimacy. I made the plunge into my romantic life poorly equipped in the area of intimacy.

Your personal reflections:

_____

_____

_____

_____

_____

_____

_____

_____

Stage 7: Age thirty-five to sixty-four	Stage Description
A crisis can occur when the adult moves from being generative to stagnating. The virtue learned at this stage is **care**.	• Starting a family, establishing a career, and being in a long-term relationship. • Raising kids, working productively, looking at the bigger picture, and giving back to society. • Concerns in this stage can cause feelings of stagnation and unproductiveness.

My personal reflections:

I had a huge amount of meaning and purpose in my life. I had a career in which I excelled and I had my son at age thirty-five, which brought further meaning and purpose at this stage. This is also when my marriage ended, because our values were out of alignment. My marriage ended when we no longer could meet each other's needs. He wanted to stay a single man and I wanted to evolve into the family stage.

Your personal reflections:

_____

_____

_____

_____

_____

_____

Stage 8: Age sixty-five and over	Stage Description
A crisis can occur when the senior moves from integrity to despair. The virtue learned at this stage is **wisdom**.	• Slowing down part of life. • Seniors decrease productivity and retire. Review accomplishments and develop either integrity or despair; despair can lead to anxiety and depression.

Maslow's Hierarchy of Needs

Maslow's Hierarchy of Needs is a theory about motivation. The basis of the theory is that basic levels of needs must be met before individuals will focus on higher-level needs. In turn, Piaget's, Erikson's, and Maslow's theories combine to highlight the ultimate need, which is being in a relationship. As mammals, we cannot live in isolation—we are wired for connection. Our stages in life teach us to be in a relationship, which is one of the highest needs in our existence as humans .

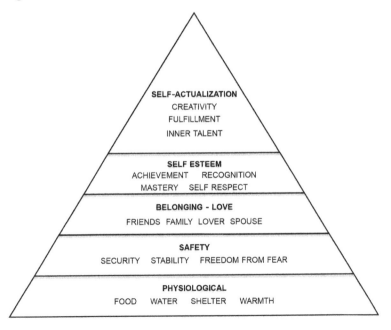

While reviewing my life, I assessed all the personal connections I had with the people so I could get a sense of where my relationship skills fell along a continuum. We typically try to develop relationships that fit our needs. Our early primary attachment with our parents basically sets the tone for these needs. As the child grows, the parents typically evolve and let the children draw the connection themselves, which builds up their autonomy. However, this is not always the case because not every child is born into a functional, caring family.

I assessed the following types of relationships: family, intimate, friendships, and career- or self-development. I found these types of relationships to have the most impact on both my life and the lives of my clients.

Relationship Likert Scale

On a scale of 1 through 10, with 1 being toxic and 10 being excellent, rate each of these relationships in your life:

Family Relationships:

1	2	3	4	5	6	7	8	9	10

Intimate Relationships:

1	2	3	4	5	6	7	8	9	10

Friendships:

1	2	3	4	5	6	7	8	9	10

Career- or Self-Development:

1	2	3	4	5	6	7	8	9	10

This will give you a score for each of your relationship areas. Scores ranging between 1 and 5 may indicate an area you need to work on and that you may benefit from seeking help or counselling in that area. Scores ranging between 5 and 10 suggest some positive core elements in those relationships.

To tabulate your final score in the relationship area, take the rating from each relationship type and add them together.

- Scores in the 5–10 range: **Good**
- Scores in the 2–5 range: **Bad**
- Scores of 1 and under: **Ugly**

Good

Your life choices are in line with what you value, your beliefs, and your assumptions. Relationships are flowing for you. There may be times when things are not going well, but you have the ability to manage your needs when things are not going well. Overall, the core elements for happiness exist in this relationship.

Bad

Your life choices may potentially still fit, but they are not totally in line with your values, beliefs, and assumptions. Your needs are not being considered or met in this relationship. You will need to use your skills to make the necessary changes in your relationships. If the skills are not there then it may be necessary to get the right type of assistance to learn these skills so that you can create the necessary changes.

Ugly

These life choices are totally out of alignment with your values, beliefs, and assumptions. "Ugly" decisions are dysfunctional and can be abusive. In this type of relationship, your needs are neglected. In this relationship, it does not matter what your needs are because they will not be met most of the time.

The final tabulation of the above will be a snapshot of the "good," "bad," and "ugly" areas of your life. The good reveals the areas where you are happy. Focus on the bad areas and the ugly habits you need to eliminate immediately.

Chapter 2:
The Stages in Your Life

My life was impacted by so many variables by the time I started to make significant life choices at age eleven. I went through the cognitive stages according to Piaget, but my inability to feel completely safe impaired the things that I processed at this stage. In accordance with Piaget's Sensorimotor Stage, my ability to impact my environment was impaired. Could I really impact the environment in the necessary way to acquire the thought process that I would need to manage this stage? According to Erikson's Stage of Development, my ability to distinguish trust from mistrust was not developed. For example, how does a child get through this phase successfully with uncertainty and unrest at home? In essence, my ability to decipher what was good for me relationally was impaired. In reviewing Maslow's Hierarchy of Needs, my safety, love, belonging, and esteem were impacted from the onset and, in turn, my motivation and abilities were skewed so I could not reach my higher-level needs.

Ideally, all the necessary elements must exist if we are to evolve into the individual we need to be. However, if core elements are missing in our lives, such as safety, then our ability to make choices about safety is skewed, and our path adjusts to compensate for that lack in our environment. The impacts of the different theorists are important to consider as a framework. If a child does not have food and water, then according to Maslow, it is difficult for the child to really consider safety and security. If children cannot explore, then they are unable to cognitively develop to a point where they can think abstractly and make more adult decisions. They are limited to black and white thinking, which they acquired at an earlier stage of development. If a child does not have safety, then how does the child develop a sense of self or trust? This is very difficult for the safety-deprived child to achieve, even in a secure and intimate relationship.

The cognitive and developmental stages of our lives are based on our immediate environment. Were you brought up in a stable caring environment or was there a lot of uncertainty? Based on your initial environment, you can start to understand how your thinking processes developed. For example, did you feel that you could explore freely and could this have influenced your view of the world? Did you feel safe and secure enough to really be able to explore the biggest questions in your life: "Who are you?" "What do you like? What do you not like?" Were you able to feel competent in your life? This is validated by the choices that you were allowed to make at each developmental stage of your life.

If you were born into a safe and secure environment where all your needs were, and still are, met on a continual basis, then your view of the world is that it is safe and secure. You are likely willing to go out there and take on each and every task that is presented to you. If one feels competent and capable of taking on all challenges, then life is a great challenge to be explored. However, if a lot of core variables are uncertain in your life, then your thoughts, actions, and interactions related to the world often become skewed. You may think the world is a scary, uncertain place and a space to be feared. In later life you are unable to listen with an uncluttered mind due to impairments in your early childhood development.

In the next chapter I will discuss how the cognitive and developmental stages impacted my body, thoughts, and emotional alignment. In turn, be prepared to answer questions at the end of the chapter to see how these stages have influenced your own life.

Check-In Questions

How happy are you with your life?

Do you feel that your life is the way you want it to be?

When you think of the choices that you have made in your life, do they align with all your values?

Are there often times when you wonder why you made the choices that did? Do you think only of others or do you think of yourself when you make decisions in life?

When you make decisions in your life, what is your process? Do you check in with yourself or do you do what you feel others need, ignoring what is best for you.

Chapter 3:
Relating My Thoughts, Body, and Emotional Alignment to the Stages

When I consider my thoughts, feelings, and behaviours, it is important to reflect on some of the psychological theories and how my environment may have impaired my ability to evolve in ways that I would have evolved in an ideal environment free of stressors. As I review Erikson's Psychosocial Developmental Stages, it becomes obvious that these stressors have affected my life.

In the early years of my life, I should have been developing a real sense of trust and caregivers should have provided reliability, care, and affection. Instead, my environment was fraught with inconsistency and chaos. I know both my parents cared for my siblings and me, but the issues in their marriage often preceded our need for safety. According to Maslow, my basic needs for food, warmth, and shelter were met, but the issue of safety was not. Cognitive theorist Piaget would say the elements I mastered at this Sensorimotor Stage were an understanding that I existed in separation from another, that I would impact things, and things continued to happen even when I couldn't see them.

At the Sensorimotor Stage, I started developing cognitively, but I doubt that I was able to impact others on a consistent basis. Overall, one can spot the glaring holes in my early development. If I had had the necessary environment to naturally develop trust, how would that have impacted my life and the choices I made? In an ideal environment, I would have focused internally instead of externally, as I did. Instead of figuring out that I needed to gain a real sense of self, I was too pre-occupied with what I needed from my external environment to be safe. Therefore, I missed a lot of key developmental markers that would have allowed me to figure out who I was and that I really needed to live life on my own terms.

As I look at trust (the pervasive concern affecting close intimate relationships in my life), it now makes complete sense that I developed blind spots in the choices I made regarding the people I allowed into my life. In accordance with Maslow, if safety and security haven't been achieved, then it is increasingly difficult to evolve through our existential needs. Because I did not really know what safety and security were supposed to feel and look like at a young age, I was ill-equipped to make healthy choices in relationships. Since I didn't feel safe emotionally and spiritually, it was tough to move up to the other stages of esteem (confidence, respect of self and others, self-actualization where one can be creative, spontaneous, and free to listen to the voice of our deep inner being).

Other key concerns to consider are the various stages of thinking and psychosocial development as I evolved into a young adult. According to Erikson, from age two I was dealing with the issue of autonomy versus shame and doubt. I learned about my physical skills and my success brought independence. I had the opportunity to manoeuvre a little at this stage, but not from a free mindset that would have allowed me to explore and evolve as I needed to. Therefore, as I evolved, both psychologically and cognitively, I learnt the past, present, and future in my cognitive processes and eventually moved on into abstract thinking. However, fear was my perpetual backdrop. Subsequently, because of that fear, I couldn't focus on all the things that I needed in order to develop a healthy sense of self and self-esteem.

How did I learn to allow my mind to be completely free and present so that I could learn the concepts of abstract thinking? I was very distracted in my classes at a young age. I was often absent mentally, but I didn't realize that it was because of what was happening at home. I thought I just didn't like school.

In primary school I was lucky to be academically inclined. I excelled at an early age, but it definitely wasn't easy. As I ploughed through my academic life, tracking became a concern at times. It wasn't because of the subject's difficulty; I simply felt overwhelmed with new information and retreated into my internal world of hyper-arousal. It was in that internal world that I haphazardly listened. My attention was minimal at best when I retreated into the abyss of my thoughts. Not being present, I felt stupid at times and, in turn, listened less. Ultimately, this impacted my ability to do well, even though I had the cognitive aptitude.

I may have misinterpreted a lot of things because of my inability to stay present and to evolve into the person that I needed to be. My ability to listen to my body, which almost always has all the answers to life's questions, has been the most impacted. My inability to stay present impacted so many things. Without free movement to learn through the senses my primary Sensorimotor Stage was impacted by the lack of safety. In turn, this impacted my higher logical thought and my ability to develop trust. If I wasn't encouraged, I might have developed shame and doubt about my abilities.

I was ignorant of my ability to listen to what was in my best interest for my relationships. I made a lot of significant choices with limited knowledge of what a healthy relationship should feel and look like. In the back of my mind I thought I would end up in a big home with a young boy and this actually became my reality. Overall, my reality was dictated by a lot of issues from my past. Since my primary relationships were not healthy in the long term, I didn't know how to recognize the thoughts, feelings, and body sensations that weren't right for me.

According to Piaget's Cognitive Theory, our thoughts evolve with each stage and age. The type of relationship I chose was based on the preoperational stage—the ability to see only black and white. There was no grey area; there was only one choice or the other. Had I learned that there was so much more to know before making choices in my life, I could have saved myself a lot of heartache. At the end of the day, I glossed over most of the microscopic details because I overemphasized that if there wasn't abuse or infidelity, then everything would fall into place. I needed to learn to listen to my senses in order to know what things would feel like in my body when I was in a safe and secure relationship. This was something that I completely missed. In the end, I picked a partner solely based on my concept of safety. I made a choice based on my inept concept of *healthy*.

As I look back, I realize that I ignored signs that things weren't going right in my primary relationships. There were many reasons, but the most pervasive one was my fear of not having safety and security. I was so wrapped up in making sure that I wouldn't have to be alone that I made a choice in my most intimate relationship based on that limited knowledge. I needed to ensure that I knew what trust looked like and felt like for me according to Erikson's stages. Inevitably, I had a working concept of what trust was like, but really did not know what trust was or what it felt like. I knew that I lacked trust in the family I grew up in, but that was it. All in all, I did not know what I needed to be safe and secure, so was incapable of understanding the concept of trust within an intimate relationship. In essence, if you do not have a safer harbour within yourself, then how do you know what it should be like with another person?

In retrospect, I also realize that unless I had a partner who was equally willing to be emotionally mature and work through things, my long-term relationship was eventually doomed. How did I choose my partner? Well, not to sound too superficial, but he had to be cute, lighthearted, fun, emotionally available, and faithful. These were my main criteria, but there were things I should have further explored, and by the time I did it was far too late. According to Maslow's theory I could not get to love and self-esteem without meeting my basic needs for safety and security. Without this understanding, my working concept for a partner lacked any real depth other than the absence of violence and infidelity.

I picked the opposite of what I had experienced in my primary home, growing up. I picked someone who was fun and not critical. He loved me unconditionally and I thought that emotionally and spiritually he would be there for me. I ensured that we made something special out of what we had found so young. Were we ready to commit? In retrospect I don't think we actually were ready, but he brought with him a lot of what that I needed when I met him. So, my need for safety and security was the corner-stone of my choices, according to Maslow. I looked for someone who could provide the security I had not found in my own home, growing up. Even though I looked for security in my partner, I only had a limited and developmentally skewed knowledge of what that should actually look and feel like. My self-esteem was externally based on how others made me feel instead of on what I needed to feel.

My choice of a mate didn't withstand the test of time because of some things that I thought were unimportant at the time; however, they were key.

I love my family, and my biggest disillusionment about my twenty-two-year marriage was when he said that he didn't want kids. He told me that he had made that clear when we first met, but as I remember it, this was not clearly articulated.

Our first step into a therapist's office was when this core difference raised its ugly head. Our lives shifted from a life of fulfillment to one of complete sadness. I allowed him to push off my needs until I finally said that we needed to deal with this difference. I had made a great choice for a "play partner" in the earlier part of my life, but I had not chosen a man who wanted a family. I needed someone who had the same long-term view of a healthy, satisfying relationship. Unfortunately, his view of his needs was like mine: shortsighted. I did not understand the latter stages of life, such as Intimacy and Isolation, when I was in my twenties. At this stage, should someone not find intimacy then there is a sense of isolation, and this is what I felt. This was the stage that my marriage could not get past. I wanted connection and my partner could not provide this for me. So I had feelings of isolation.

As Erikson claims, from twelve through eighteen years of age is when I needed to develop a sense of self and personal identity, but instead I was more focused on being safe and secure in my crumbling relationship. I thought I was being true to myself, but I developed a weak sense of self and I lost track of what I needed in a relationship. At the age of eighteen, I met someone, but I was too young to evaluate the psychological factors of a relationship. I needed to figure out what I needed to make me safe. I guess I did a relatively good job considering I was so young.

I needed to figure out what friendship, family, and sexual intimacy meant to me in the long term versus the short term. In order to achieve an actualized state (a state where one's personal potential becomes a possibility), I should have spent reflective time with myself. However, I wonder where that wisdom would have come from, because I had no guidance myself. Symbolically, I was a rudderless ship looking for a safe harbour, which I eventually thought I had found and, dysfunctional as it was, I stayed there until I learned my life lessons and realized it was time to move on. Overall, I developed a skewed view of connection because I had to disconnect to keep myself physically and emotionally safe. In turn, this gave me a concrete short-term emotional relationship that could not withstand the test of the Generative versus Stagnation period (age thirty-five through sixty-five). My partner lacked meaning and purpose, so the feeling of stagnation ended the relationship after twenty-two years of marriage.

In the next three chapters, I will discuss my Child Years, Teen Years, and Adulthood and how I developed my blueprint in each of these stages.

I now ask you to challenge yourself to be introspective about your thoughts, feelings, and behaviours. In answering these questions, I hope you can look at the overall picture of your life. Next, you should examine your life in relation to the three theorists in Chapter 2 and see how they apply to the overall blueprint of your life. I hope that you can look at your early life as though you're a bit of a detective. Look at the strengths and limitations of your early childhood and create an initial frame to help you work your way through our journey of your blueprint.

Check-In Questions

How did your life circumstances impact your thoughts, feelings, and behaviours?

Do you understand how things in your life may affect how you connect to yourself, to others close to you, and to the world?

What developmental issues may have impacted your thoughts, feelings, and behaviours in your life?

Are there pervasive thoughts that often appear in your life? If so, what are they?

What areas of your life do these thoughts take you to?

How often do you take the time to clear your thoughts and feelings so you can reflect on your behaviour?

What forms of mindfulness do you practice? How do you find this helpful?

As you reflect on parts of your life, which areas have been impacted by negative life circumstances?

Are there any pervasive negative emotions that you carry with you on a continual basis? How old were you at the time that they started?

How do you know if you are making a bad decision in your life? Are there things you hear in your thoughts, in your emotions, or in your body?

CHAPTER 4:
My Childhood

I was born into a family where my parents already had three children all very close in age. My entrance into the world wasn't troubled by any health concerns. Instead, I met all the biological developmental milestones, and at times exceeded those expectations. My parents welcomed me into the world with open loving arms; however, the stressors in my life started to have an impact on me at a relatively young age. Hence, I feel that my beautiful dreams had a shroud of invisibility and hindered some of the stages of my life.

The Beginning Years

My life started on a little island called Trinidad and today I live in a city called Niagara Falls. As a little girl I was playful and fun. I quickly earned the nickname "Chatterbox." I grew up in a rural part of the island in a family of six. Our culture created a place where I felt tremendous love and there was always a sense of connection everywhere I went. In retrospect, this is how I formulated the connections I have to the community I live in today. As a child, I loved running around barefoot and playing with my siblings. There was always someone to play with and, in turn, someone to fight with! The village around me reflected a sense of community. The neighbours looked out for all the kids in the neighbourhood. I remember liking the space my parents had created for us children and the warmth I felt just being. My early childhood was filled with laughter and hours and hours of planting vegetable gardens and having garden fights. My siblings and I formed alliances and tampered with the enemies' gardens—then we would declare a truce and have a meal. I can't remember what we concocted, but I remember enjoying the teamwork and the process of putting something together. Even though there was uncertainty at a very young age I was still able to feel joy and connection to others around me. According to all the developmental stages, some core things may have been missed, but I was still able to have some fun in my early life.

My early experiences included both positive and negative things. I wonder what my brain was taking in as I reflect on the fact that only five percent of my thoughts were conscious and the rest unconscious.

As a young child I realized that to be in the moment was something special. I relished running around in the beautiful sunshine and having fun with my siblings. Unfortunately, I also realized that my environment wasn't safe. I couldn't rely on my parents to keep me safe because they were too involved in their own issues to realize that their children needed them.

I was four years old when I recognized the violence within my immediate family. What did I do? I disconnected from myself. I needed to be held and protected, but my father was absorbed in his issues and my mother was an abused woman who was dealing with her own pain.

I vividly remember the times, which are too numerous to count, when I lay in bed listening to my father hitting my mother. It was usually late at night. My father would come home and check on each and every one of us before going to bed. It would often be okay; there would be a stillness and I could fall back to sleep. Many times, however, I heard their voices rise. Shortly after, things were tossed around and then total chaos would erupt. Then all six of us children were up, yelling and screaming, as my father hit my mother.

I can recall my thoughts, feelings, and body sensations as if they are occurring right now. I believed life was going to be bad; I hoped that my father wouldn't drink too much and I hoped that my mom wouldn't say too much to him. These thoughts filled my mind again and again.

I often felt sadness, despair, horror, anger, disillusionment, and disdain towards my father and my body responded to my feelings. My heart would pound. My stomach would flutter. My feet and hands would go cold and I would feel a surge of energy all over my body. At an early age I learned to disconnect from normalcy and focus on protecting myself from danger. Due to the violence in our home, my siblings and I didn't focus on our own emotional needs.

According to sensorimotor psychotherapy, children who grow up with exposure to violence become hypervigilant, which means that they struggle every day, detecting threats on a constant basis.

> "If clinicians fail to look through a trauma lens and to conceptualize client problems as related possibly to current or past trauma, they may fail to see that trauma victims, young and old, organize much of their lives around repetitive patterns of reliving and warding off traumatic memories, reminders, and affects." (Kathleen Moroz, "The Effects of Psychological Trauma on Children and Adolescents" 2005)

What bodily sensation told me I needed to be hyper-aware of the relationships in my life? From as early as I can remember, when I heard loud voices, I looked around to make sure that I was safe. I looked first for safety and security. I disconnected from my thoughts and feelings. Because of the violence in my parents' marriage, my primary concern was survival. Therefore, I was hypersensitive to stressors that made me feel unsafe and I was always on guard. I couldn't learn to listen to my needs. As a result, I couldn't figure out what I needed in order to acquire a healthy sense of self or individuation from the primary family I was born into.

My fragmented sense of self developed in response to these early stressors. Survival was key. I couldn't afford to trust and relax or explore what I thought or what interested me.

Without a secure space to go to in my mother, who was my primary attachment figure, I developed a poor self-image and in turn I connected with someone who had the same issues. I ignored so many signals in my body that I should have listened to. Thankfully, I now understand why I stayed in the horrible situation that I did for so long.

My body sent constant messages to me. I suffered from sleeplessness. My thoughts raced and I had hyper-arousal symptoms, such as an accelerated heart and fluttering stomach, but I ignored these messages because I didn't think they were a symptom of my environment. As a child, I naturally listened to my body. When we are born we cry for our primary caregiver and our needs are met. As children, this is our only means of survival, so we naturally learn to get what we want by listening to our bodily needs.

As I reflect on the different theories of early childhood development this seems automatic. In everyday society when we are out and about, we naturally react to the sound of a baby crying. I think this is our natural biological instinct to take care of others.

It is undeniably obvious in my family photos when I started to disconnect from what I felt. In my baby pictures I had the biggest grin that ran from ear to ear, very much like the one that I see clearly in my son today. However, in my family album there was a marked change in my smile as I got older. That smile became almost non-existent and my body language reflected sadness. My body did not steer me wrong as a natural human being, but listening became too painful.

My chaos was real as a child. I have memories of always having to be on guard and a child is not meant to be on guard. Children learn to trust, and once they listen to their bodies, they vocalize their needs knowing that their needs will be met.

When a secure caregiver consistently meets a child's needs, the child evolves into the person they are naturally meant to be. However, if a child's sense of safety and security is impaired by chaos and violence, normal development is disrupted. Therefore, when I was young, I couldn't listen to what I needed. I learned to disconnect from my body, which actually stored all the information I needed to proceed through the normal developmental stages of child.

When my dad came home at night, when I heard the sound of the door closing and the loud screams of my mother, I felt scared, overwhelmed, and unsafe. I wanted to escape my reality. This altered my perception of my little world and the world at large. I needed some comfort, but it wasn't possible. Instead, my siblings and I got up in the middle of the night and got in the middle of the physical conflict to stop the escalation of our parents' fights. We acted as a physical shield. We protected our mother from our father and prayed that our intervention would stop their conflict.

Since I was the middle child, I felt left out at times. The oldest sibling was given special attention and the smallest was spoiled rotten. My parents brought many problems from their immediate families with them. They were not well equipped to start a life together and much less equipped to take care of six children—all under the age of ten.

My mother came from a family where she witnessed a lot of abuse and alcoholism. She was born into a family of eleven children; she was the baby girl. On the other hand, my father was the *parentified* child. His parents looked up to him as though he was their parent. He took on the role of a caretaker at the young age of fourteen and found employment so he could help his cane farmer parents raise his siblings.

My parents came together because they wanted the same thing. They loved their children but they didn't have the necessary life skills to manoeuvre through the minefield of life or to create a healthy relationship with each other and the six young children under foot. They both wanted to be cared for, but they didn't know how their needs could be met. Ultimately, this led to the early violence and infidelity that I witnessed as a child. At a very young age I started to focus on the concerns that permeated my early life. I was always on guard for the next fight that would take place in my family home.

In my hypersensitivity towards my parents' issues, I couldn't focus on what I needed because my primary caregivers couldn't give me that. My thoughts, feelings, and behaviours were impacted very early by my exposure to a lot of adult concerns. I loved my parents dearly, but recognized I needed to rely on myself, which wasn't good for my development. As early as four, I started to telegraph the things I needed in my life, but instead of focusing on what I needed, I was busy focusing on my parents.

According to each of the different psychosocial child development stages outlined in Chapter 1, my environment did not allow the progression of some key developmental markers. I believe my mother tried her best to meet my needs, but she couldn't cope due to the chaos that already existed in her world. She had three young children and a baby, and I can only assume she did her best to meet my needs—but against the prevailing backdrop of uncertainty. According to Erikson, inconsistent caregivers may struggle from the fear and belief that their world is inconsistent and unpredictable.

I can only assume that I could not stop to listen to what I needed due to the immense amount of stress I was born into. When I disconnected from my thoughts and feelings, I did not cope. I disconnected when my marriage started to fall apart, I didn't listen to my thoughts and feelings. Often I couldn't eat, sleep, or focus, but I still pushed through by using the frame that things weren't as bad as I thought. I ignored my bodily cues. I ignored the steadily intensifying issues, which were all of the issues that I had tried to ignore as a child. I repeated the patterns of my past—the very patterns that I had dreaded throughout my life.

At this moment in time, it is clear to me how much I wanted to feel safe and secure. I often unplugged from myself to create a story—one based on fairy tales where I could be perfectly happy and where all my needs met could be met and everyone in my life could be healthy and mature. It was a place where I had all the variables I needed; however, the one key variable that I needed to pay attention to was my body.

Chapter 4

Check-In Questions

Reflect on your family of origin. How would you describe your relationship with your parents? And siblings?

How many siblings did you have and what order were you in the family?

Did this order in the family affect how you were treated compared to the others?

Who was the emotional keeper of the family?

Did both parents play an equal role in parenting?

How did your father demonstrate affection? And your mother?

How did their parenting styles impact how you got your needs met as a child?

Did one of your parents have an addiction?

Was there any type of violence or abuse? If so, how did that impact you and your family system?

Did you go to the same schools as your peers in your early years? If so, what was that like for you?

Or did you move a lot and how did that affect you, your family, and your early friendships?

Were there a lot of family rules? If so, outline them and explore where they started.

Were these rules helpful or harmful to your early development?

CHAPTER 5:
My Teen Years

What were my earliest experiences with relationships? My first exposure to relationships was to my parents' relationship. When I look back on my parents and their relationship, I know they loved each other no matter how dysfunctional their relationship was. From a very young age I saw the love between them, but this was also entangled with chaos. As I grew into my teens and developed reasoning, I knew and felt the love and care they had for me, but I also saw a relationship fraught with discord.

I learned early on that there was uncertainty in life and in relationships in general. I also knew I wanted to receive love, so I picked my partners based on what I thought was ideal. I knew my father wasn't ideal, so I started to think of the qualities I would need in a great partner. I wanted someone who would make me feel like the centre of his universe. I needed someone who was emotionally and physically available for me and had qualities that my father and other men in my culture lacked.

I wanted someone who came from a cultural background and upbringing that was different from my own. I felt my culture was very patriarchal, and so I invested deeply in someone who could treat me as his equal. I wanted someone who was fun and who could stay in the moment; someone I could grow with. Ideally, I saw myself with a professional, hard-working man who would make me his priority.

My grandfather was a kind gentle man. He was intelligent and loving, but it was glaringly obvious that my grandmother was in charge of the family. I loved my grandfather, but I wanted someone who could be my equal in every sense of the word. My culture's values implied that men couldn't be relied upon to be consistent or treat women with equality. There was a lot of infidelity and physical abuse. My ideal mate seemed to be the polar opposite from the men in my life—especially from my father. As a child I knew what I wanted, and I was bound and determined to achieve my results. I knew what I didn't want. I thought a lot about what my partner's attributes should not be: he shouldn't be unfaithful, he shouldn't be emotionally or physically abusive, he shouldn't be domineering or mean, he shouldn't be emotionally immature, he shouldn't drink and party with his friends all the time, he should never put another woman ahead of me, and he should never be condescending towards me. Away I went with my ideal list. I felt I was clear in what I wanted because I knew on a conscious level what I didn't want.

When I think back to my first crush in primary school, the boy had to be cute and he needed to treat me well of course. I remember my very first smooch! It was so cute and innocent. I thought I was in love. My view at that stage was ideal. As long as they loved me, things would work out. Doesn't love make the world go around?

In my Cinderella story, I wanted my prince to be ideal. I see how the media influenced me. I relished my weekly shows where I dreamed of the ideal man. I daydreamed that I wouldn't be like my mother who had made a horrible choice in her partner.

When I watched *Little House on the Prairie* and *Eight is Enough*, I thought, *Bingo! Here's the kind of ideal man I want*. The leading men in these shows were thoughtful, kind, considerate, and loving. They also showed concern for their partners and families. I had found the perfect template. All I needed to do was go out there and find my Mr. Perfect. Of course, he was just waiting for me to appear.

There are different theories about how we pick our ideal mate. In reviewing various theories, I recognize that I formulated my blueprint of the ideal mate from The Ideal Mate Theory. Basically, I formed my vision of a mate based on my list of ideal characteristics. In other words, the concept of Love at First Sight worked for me. Generally, I believed that I would pick my mate from my own social network: same schools, socio-economic background, and the like. They were caring and kind, but most of all they fell in love with me.

There are many varying descriptions of the ideal mate selection. According to Freud, we select mates who reflect the characteristics of the opposite sex parent. I thought I picked someone completely the opposite of my father—but did I? In my collection of ideal traits for my perfect partner, I consciously knew what I didn't want, but on the other hand, I also knew what I wanted. I specifically chose to not date anyone who had any traits that vaguely reminded me of my father. In reviewing psychological theories like Freud's, I definitely didn't fit his definition of the ideal partner. Whoever I dated, he wasn't going to be anything like my dad.

We all pick our ideal mates based on some particular formula that we create in our mind. I cited several theorists that I used to formulate my supposedly ideal blueprint. There are numerous other theories; for example, the theory of natural selection suggests that men pick partners who can bear their babies and women pick men who will be good providers. In this theory, people choose partners to ensure the viability of future generations. Therefore, not only do people pick good partners for themselves, but they also ensure that they make healthy babies, and that the couple stays together to ensure the viability of their children.

American psychologist David Buss suggests that men pick mates for sexual attraction and women pick for success. The real question is at which age do we formulate this ideal? I believe I formulated my ideal at the age of eleven or twelve. Unconsciously, I defined my choices.

The following questions will relate back to why we choose the mates we do.

Check-In Questions

Reflect back on your first love relationship. What were the qualities that attracted you to that relationship?

Describe your first emotional relationship. How long did it last? Who ended the relationship and why?

What qualities do you look for in a relationship? Itemize a list of these qualities and reflect why each quality is important to you and why.

Are there any similar patterns that you see in your partners? Explore these patterns. When did they start and are they still there in your current relationship?

How do you get your emotional, physical, psychological, and spiritual needs met in your relationships?

How do you know that you are in a healthy relationship?

What are the indicators that tell you that this is right for you?

What does it look like, feel like and how does this play through in your relationship?

CHAPTER 6:
Adulthood

Early Adulthood:
The Learning Years

Life often becomes more real to us as we get older. We are forced to take a closer look at our lives when things are not working for us because this means that at least one area of life is out of alignment with our values. We become wiser as we age, but if the people in our lives do not want the same things that we do, then we need to make decisions that keep us true to our ego identity or sense of self.

In my immediate family, once I hit early adulthood I recognized my parents weren't the perfect human beings I wanted them to be. My father was a sweet, caring man, but at times he was tyrannical in nature. My mother invested in being the best mother possible, but as I grew older, I recognized her identity wasn't working well for her. My mother believed that if she married the man she loved that everything would work out because love conquers all. When it became clear that love was not going to conquer, it was difficult for her to come to terms with this reality. My mother tried to hide her pain by focusing on her children but soon she started to realize that her marriage was getting worse. My family life started to show its cracks. I cannot determine exactly how old I was when I realized he was physically abusing her.

This abuse was a long-term pattern, but it was not until I was an adult that I recognized it. According to Erikson's theory, during the stage of Intimacy versus Isolation (ages twenty through thirty-four) is when we start to recognize ongoing concerns with connection. I realized that my parents had real issues in their marriage when I started my intimate relationship. In my relationship there was some conflict but nothing like I had witnessed between my parents throughout my life with them. This is typical because prior to this stage of development, many people may not have had an ongoing solid, intimate relationship.

As a child, my world and all my beautiful bonds of connection were shattered right before my eyes. How does one cope with this? I loved my father and mother so much. My confusion was immense as a small child. Developmentally, I thought that when you loved someone you would never hurt them; hence, my confusion in the area of relationships. My family life framed my conscious and unconscious choices in my own intimate relationships in early adulthood and throughout my life. I learned early that one should be guarded in life so as to avoid being hurt.

Throughout my teen years I was really angry at the world—especially with my dad. How could the man who I loved cause me so much pain? If I had the safety and security of a securely attached father, then I would have gained an inner picture of what it would be like to be loved unconditionally by a man, but instead I had the opposite. I never wanted to pick a man like my father, but in actuality I did not know what unconditional love from a man would look and feel like. If there was a remote possibility that someone I liked could in any way be like my dad, then he was gone.

From the time I began to date, I was hypersensitive to the qualities of abusive relationships. If I became close to someone and thought they were going to leave me, I left them before they could leave me. I got out of a lot of potentially good relationships from the fear of getting hurt, but unfortunately I didn't recognize the pattern until much later. Another pattern that started to show itself, which I did not recognize until a lot later, was that I was picking partners who inevitability ended up being unfaithful. I was hyper-vigilant about trust, but I still picked men who were unfaithful. In retrospect, I wasn't attracted to the men who would have been faithful. My unconsciousness was raising its ugly head and I didn't recognize the signs. I was unconsciously attracted the very thing that I was most concerned about.

Who was the ideal mate I chose for myself? He was smart, good looking, and from the same socio-economic background as me. He appeared to have been raised in the same cultural milieu as myself. He was Canadian. This was a conscious choice I made because of my early cultural experience. I viewed my culture as patriarchal. Most of the males were domineering and controlling in my experience and women took on traditional roles as mothers and caregivers. When I looked around at my culture and my family, I did not see examples of the male that I wanted to start my life with. The men around me were mostly abusive, self-centered infidels with a view that women were not their equal. My choice of mate has the same kind of ambition and drive as myself, and most of all, since we met at age eighteen he didn't have any additional baggage at that time that would add stress to my life.

Continuing with my ideal checklist, he made me laugh, he appeared to be emotionally available, he wasn't physically abusive, and he appeared to come from a nice family. My decision was made. I had found my knight in shining armour at the young and quite naive age of eighteen. At that point, I thought that my life was complete and therefore, I went on to create the other parts of my ideal life. With everything else seemingly in place, it was time to fall in love and we did. After all, I had already gone through multiple relationships by this tender age—surely I knew a good thing when I saw it. I had met the man that would be my life mate at university. I recall his tenderness, or in retrospect, his innocence, or perhaps I should say his lack of maturity. He was caring and warm and he definitely didn't resemble my dad.

When I was twenty-one years old, the relationship with my immediate family was quite strained. At this point in my life I felt that I had definitely figured things out. I had kept a physical distance from my primary family and moved far away from the pain that I resented so much. I moved to a small town with someone who I knew would never hurt me, but as life proceeded, he did. Consciously, I made a commitment to someone whom I was madly in love with. I felt this choice would give me a new lease on a new life, far away from the prison cell of my painful childhood, teens, and early adulthood.

During my twenties, I built a life where I followed my dreams of having a career. I enjoyed the security of our flourishing relationship and I was able to achieve my career objectives with a lot of hard work and relative ease. I enjoyed the pleasures of connecting with my new in-laws. Compared to my family, they were reserved, but they also seemed to be nice people. The key variable was an absence of abuse. I looked at them through a different lens. While my love for my partner deepened so did his love for me. Our love expanded from an early primary state to a place where we took care of each other. We kept each other safe both physically and emotionally. His family wasn't devoid of their problems, but compared to my family they satisfied what my young heart needed at the time. My partner and I were married, and I believed that all the insanity was in my past—or so I thought. I revelled in my marital life and I ignored a lot of signs to which I should have paid heed. However, it was so much better than what I had come from. I ignored my inner voice, which said that the relationship wasn't going to last. While all this was going on, the relationship with my primary family faded in the distance.

I still acted as my mother's rescuer and continued to hate my father. I lived far away and the beauty of distance is that it acts as the ideal buffer. I still received chaotic phone calls and I was constantly wrapped up in the drama, but my new family helped me to manage the maelstrom of my abusive past.

I focused on my new life and assured myself that nothing would get in my way of having a great life in Niagara Falls. I had a lot of fun with my new love. We played and we explored, and this life situation taught me so many life lessons. I learned about safety and security from this relationship. I was able to love unconditionally. I learned to allow myself to be vulnerable. I allowed myself to receive love—even though I was a bit guarded at first. With time, maturity, and consistency I allowed myself to receive real love. In this space I inwardly blossomed. Some of these personal inner qualities are still evident today, and when I reflect back this was a significant period of growth in my life. From the frame of love, I grew both professionally and personally.

Life Stage Thirty-Five Plus
Middle Adulthood: The "Ugly" Years

Time serves many purposes. Time allows things to be uncovered, and with the right conditions they come into fruition. In my thirties I worked arduously, building my career and preparing with my partner to have a family. Then came the pain of encountering the things that were hidden for years. As a couple we had accomplished so many things. We created our lives together, we grew up together, and the next logical step in my eyes was to start a family. I started broaching the subject with my partner and he deflected it. He created every excuse in the book; we didn't have the right house, we weren't settled in our careers, we didn't have enough money, and on he went. My real disillusionment started when I realized that there was trouble in paradise. We were able to resolve our concerns, but this issue wasn't one we could solve on our own, so we went to therapy.

In therapy, I realized that my partner didn't want to have children and even to consider having children was a difficult step for him. As we sought assistance, he acted more developmentally regressive. This major life decision was significant in our lives. This was the turning point for me in recognizing that we had some major differences in our values and what we wanted in our lives. We were both unhappy and even though counselling was supposed to help it did not.

Instead, counselling brought to light all the issues I had ignored for years. My partner had a traumatic loss in his past: the sudden death of his father. Therefore, he never wanted to get close to anyone again. For him, on an unconscious level, having a child would bring him too close to vulnerability again, a state that was too painful to revisit. My partner loved me dearly, but he was able to keep me emotionally distanced so that he couldn't get hurt. Then I—the love of his life—decided that either we make the decision to have a family or we end the marriage.

Counselling was tough. We started to discuss the issues I believed to be acceptable, such as having children and planning for the future, but my partner emotionally backed away from me. After a while, he admitted that he was scared to start a family, but he also loved me so much that he decided to deal with his concerns of vulnerability and have a family. I was so happy and I thought that my partner was too, but the issue still appeared to be difficult for him. One of my first clues was when we went to our doctor's appointment to verify the pregnancy.

My partner appeared confused and kept asking the doctor, "Are you sure she is pregnant?"

I tried to ignore his response. I treated it as one of mass hysteria and thought it would pass. What was I supposed to do other than assume this was a guy's regular response to having a baby? Guys usually act oddly when they find out their wife is pregnant for the first time. In the back of my mind, the fact that we were in our mid-thirties made me realize that this was an abnormal response. I then began to question what else he was hiding. The answer to this question was a lot.

I thought that I had chosen well. Over fifteen years there were bumps along the way, but this new hurdle of the decision to start a family appeared to be uglier than most erupting volcanoes. For me, my issue with becoming emotionally vulnerable was about to come to fruition. I was pregnant and the fear of God had started to enter my partner's head. This child represented his greatest fear: that of being completely vulnerable to another human being. This was something he hadn't had to deal with since tragically losing his dad at the age of fifteen.

How did I miss this concern in my partner? Did I see the signs and ignore them because of my own abandonment issues? I saw the signs when we were dating, but I thought he was quite young and that these fears would no longer be issues as he matured. His decisions about the future always involved the two of us, but in an egocentric way they were devoid of any room for a family. My history of coming from a large family gave me an unconscious validation that I would have a family of my own. However, when trauma strikes a young man who loses his father, how does he cope? He learned to be ultra-independent, and in the end, this left no room for a family. Sharing me with a child became too much.

During my pregnancy, this sweet man whom I so fondly loved started to stay out late, drank to excess, and hung out with men who were less than desirable. I assumed this behaviour was a result of his struggle with the process of becoming a father; meanwhile, I stifled my feelings of abandonment. I wondered how this man—who was passionate about me—could do this to me? I believed it to be a temporary phase that would soon pass. My naivety didn't serve me well at this point in the game.

Throughout my pregnancy, our relationship continued to decline. At this point I actually became happier as the life grew inside me. I felt so much love for my unborn child with each inch and pound I gained. However, my partner's behaviour worsened to the point where I received the biggest clue that the deterioration of my marriage was real.

Eight months into my pregnancy I was on my way to an appointment when I fell directly on my tummy. Cars stopped and a massive chaos erupted around me. I recall lying on my back thinking that I was in labour. I went into therapist mode and stayed completely calm. I was rushed to the hospital where I was told that I was having contractions, but in the end, everything was fine for both the baby and me. In essence, once the adrenalin subsided, my fear slowly left and I felt more at ease about the welfare of my baby, but deep inside I was still fearful. Still, the doctors advised me to rest and get right back to the hospital if I had any concerns at all. My partner came to the hospital and took me home, but he told me he needed to go out. I told him I was scared and didn't want him to go far. He ignored my needs and went out drinking all night with his friends.

Deep in the core of my heart I felt really sad. I really needed my partner to be there for our unborn child and me, but he put his needs ahead of his family's needs. My deeper inner voice said that this was really bad, but I pushed on. The clues kept presenting themselves but I continually shoved them aside. My pattern of ignoring the signs in front of me became consistent from this point on in our relationship. The problems in our marriage escalated as they showed up over and over again.

The first year of our son's life was overwhelming and exhilarating all at once. The concerns I had about my partner were real and were revealed as his infantile behaviour continued. I immersed myself in mothering while my marriage fell apart. My partner started to stay out all night and our regular conflicts became more intense. At my insistence, he attended counselling but he didn't see the need to make the changes he was told that he needed to make. All he wanted was his old life back without any changes, but the variable was our new baby boy.

My first year at home with our baby was delightful. I was challenged in so many ways as a mother and I grew so much as a person. The growth I gained was an inverse of what my partner was going through. He continued to regress and live in his lies and deceit for the next year of our lives. I went back to work after a year of maternity leave. That year of our relationship wasn't the best, but I pressed on. However, his behaviour became worse. He complained incessantly that he wasn't happy babysitting while I worked. I thought I would never hear those words from my husband, but his need to focus on his world continued in a purely infantile way. There was no doubt that he loved our son, but he seemed to be very resentful of me as I resumed my corporate position out of town. In retrospect, I juggled so many things. I had a two-hour commute every day combined with the struggle of redefining myself as a competent executive. While at home, I struggled with my partner's regressive coping skills.

Life became rougher, but again I gave him the benefit of the doubt that his abandonment issues were making the adjustment of being a father difficult for him. I felt the need to be more considerate. Therefore, I put my needs and wants aside so I could focus on my family and our precious boy. My responsibilities at work were immense, but I made the transition quite fluidly into the corporate world. I worked hard to regain my position in the company and I was assigned some high corporate accounts. I felt more successful as the days went by, but my home life was beginning to cave in. My partner drank a lot and stayed out at bars when I worked late. His mother babysat our son until almost nine o'clock at night, at which point he picked up our son and arrived home just prior to my arrival. I begged and pleaded with him to stop his bad behaviour; however, I realized the situation was getting worse instead of better.

The second year of our son's life proved to be the worst year of my life. My partner's misbehaviour continued and I finally started to wonder why he staying out all night. I started to suspect infidelity, but my partner was flawless at disguising his lies. My inner voice told me I needed to get to the bottom of things. I started to think the one man who I thought would never cheat on me might actually be cheating.

One evening I went to a fondue party at my neighbour's house and when I returned home, I coerced information out of my partner. I told him how sad I felt that this life stage was so difficult for him. I said he was a great person and our special love could get us through anything. I worked on him for about an hour, at which point he divulged that he had been having an affair for the last year. The pain I felt in that moment was comparable to nothing I had ever felt in my life. I couldn't physically feel my body and I felt a part of me die inside. I sobbed for hours and hours to the point where my mother-in-law came over and retrieved our son. My partner tried to console me, but there was nothing he could do to stop this gaping wound that he had punctured in my heart.

My belief in true love and faithfulness was shattered forever. My greatest fear was realized. The man I loved was having an affair just as my dad had. I blamed myself as well, because I had consciously picked this sweetheart of a man who never saw infidelity in his family, who was caring and kind, but he did the exact same thing that broke my heart as a little girl. The one fear of my life became a reality: the love of my life had killed my love. How I was going to live through this? He apologized over and over again, but I couldn't feel or even hear his words. To this day, if I look at a photograph from that time, I can't even recall how I got there. I have a picture of myself with my son, which was taken after he mistakenly threw a toy at me and I had a bruise on my nose. This picture was the mirror into the deep psychological trauma that I had endured.

I took my son and ran away to my best friend's home in Toronto, in hopes of getting some mental respite. My best friend is in the field of psychology as I am today. I can only remember that I told her that my marriage was over, my partner had an affair, and I needed to start a new life. Both my friend and I had worked together assisting victims of a crime several years before. I went to her because she knew the field and understood me on a profound level. I even felt better by just sitting with her in silence.

Upon my return from Toronto, I reconciled with my partner. I was still in denial. I felt it would be a mistake to leave because the depth of his despair was obvious. I couldn't easily throw away fifteen years of a marriage and my son's opportunity to grow up in an intact family. I justified this with the thought that anyone is capable of making mistakes. I should have just kept on going and never looked back, but the conscious choices I made were deeply marred by the blueprint of my past. Reconciliation was definitely not easy. The pain remained between us, and my partner's behaviour continued to deteriorate. I also learned that I was capable of forgiveness but I also needed my partner to work equally as hard to rebuild trust, which did not happen. I tried hard to look past his errors in judgment and plug along in the relationship, but his bad behaviour continued. Since the affair continued, I ran away and went to Trinidad without my son.

I needed to reconnect myself to the person I was: not the wife, and not the mother.

Taking off and spending time away from my son was a very difficult thing for me to do, but as they say, "When the plane is going down, put the mask on the adult first and then assist the child."

If you put the mask on yourself first, then the odds are that you can keep oxygenated and then help your children instead of passing out while helping them. As I went away, I knew my family would take good care of my son. I needed time to regain a mental foothold on my life. I replenished myself and when I returned, I felt badly that my son would grow up in a broken home just like I did, so I decided to put my head down and work on our marriage. My tenaciousness worked wonders in other parts of my life, but definitely not in my intimate relationship. Several months later, I learnt that my husband's deceit continued. Consequently, I took all his belongings to his mother's home and told her I couldn't do this anymore—that she should tell her son I couldn't be married to him any longer.

I felt a great sense of relief, but also a sense of real sadness. I had lost my best friend, but the man I left wasn't the sweet caring man I had loved for fifteen years. This man was an imposter; he was someone who had taken his place over the years. I needed to take control of my chaotic life and create a sense of normalcy for my infant son. I dove into the deep end as I left our marriage behind, or so I thought.

During our separation, I coped by focusing on this little guy who was unaware that his circumstances had changed. I kept the house up and juggled my time between my corporate job and being the best parent I could be, all while managing the chaotic behaviour of my ex. At one point during the first eighteen months of separation, I unplugged my phone so I could sleep through the night. Sometimes I received up to thirty calls from him at a time. We interacted sporadically throughout the year, but eventually I completely disconnected from him while he spiraled further into his addictive behaviours.

I learnt my lessons, but then I had to have surgery and the fear of never waking up from the anesthetic caused me to feel that I needed to reconnect with my ex. I was afraid. If I didn't make it through the surgery, I wanted to make sure that my ex could potentially clean up his act and take over the responsibility of raising his son. I considered reconciliation with the condition that we enter marital therapy. The second round of therapy began, and the focus was mainly to discuss the conditions that were necessary for family and couple reintegration. There was some progress, and with these signs we decided he could move back into our home while the therapist felt that he should continue counselling on his own. However, within months his addictive behaviours reappeared along with his hostility and loss of emotional control.

For four excruciating years, I turned my back on my inner voice and stayed in the marriage. I tried to leave a couple of times, but I always went back. When I finally got the courage to leave again, my ex went public with the affair that he told me he had ended upon reconciliation with me. I had ignored all the signs and clues. I didn't want to believe I could be betrayed again. I consciously stayed, but something woke me up. Other than my marriage being over, the one thing that created a place of creativity and fulfillment in me was my corporate job in Toronto. However, this too started to become a place of discomfort, and just like my marriage, it slowly deteriorated. I had relished the professional role I had previously taken on ten years before. My work in that field was quite often a great place to seek relief from the depths of concerns that were glaringly obvious in my marriage. As a young therapist, I yearned to explore every facet of my field.

After delving into every arena, I recognized that I needed to pick a particular area of psychology to focus on. I loved the corporate sector of Health and Wellness, so I picked that field of specialty. I then recognized I didn't have a mentor, so I hired a coach. He helped me to look at my career objectives and where I should head next on my career path.

Within a month of working with my coach, I landed my dream job. In this new executive role, I felt totally alive. I dealt with psychological concerns that impacted different sectors and made recommendations for Health and Wellness strategies. Life was good, until several years and multiple mergers and acquisitions later, my ideal situation turned sour with the corporate directive and the supervisor. My life became a nightmare in a short period of time.

One day I realized that my planned life wasn't how I saw it any longer. The universe said to me, "It's time to wake up." By this point, a stranger on the street had physically assaulted me, I'd lost my job, and my marriage was over. On the whole, my life has not stopped changing since 11 November 2009. It was as though a mystical force said to me that it was time to make change, and along with the assault came the rapid ongoing change.

Check-In Questions

Are there qualities that you used as a frame to pick your current partner that no longer fit your frame of a healthy relationship?

In this stage of life, are there factors in your relationships that no longer work for you but you constantly ignore them because you think that they will change by themselves?

What are the current signs in your body that tell you that you are satisfied with your current relationships?

Are there certain thoughts and feelings?

What do you do to rectify these concerns when things are not going well in your relationships?

Are your emotional needs being met at this stage of life?

How did you and your partner negotiate your needs in this stage of the relationship?

CHAPTER 7:

The Body as a Messenger

As I reflect back on my blueprint and the unconscious choices that I made that impacted my life, the patterns of my disconnection are obvious. I know there is a lot of research on attachment, which states that the in-utero embryo is able to feel the stressors of the mother and the environment during pregnancy. When I think of the frame of my mother's pregnancy, it tells me that my parents really wanted another child, and they really wanted a boy. They already had two girls and a boy, and then along came me. Ultimately, there must have been a lot of disappointment in my family because I could not carry on the family name, but they told me they loved me when I was born.

Therefore, stress has a large effect on the outcome of a person's life. My mother ran back several times to her parent's home to get away from my dad, but she was explicitly given the message that this was part of married life and that she needed to go back to her husband and family. Hence, I came into the world already marred with a frame of abuse. My mother was twenty-five years old and she had already encountered horrendous beatings from my father. My environment was abusive even while I was an in-utero embryo.

The amount of protective mechanisms that my mother's system would have had to endure to ensure that she carried me to full term must have been endless. On top of that, she had to care for three young children ages three, four, and five. I often wonder what the reality was like for her when I think in terms of my own life and how different our lives were, yet how her decisions ultimately affected my own. The trauma of her stress existed in my life from the day of my conception. The cortisol that was continually poured into me via the umbilical cord had to be flowing steadily. If theorists like Gwen Dewar PhD, Biological Anthropology (Parenting Science website) are correct in stating that children learn a lot about their environment during the final five months before birth, then I learned very early that the world is a dark scary place where safety and security do not exist.

How did my cultural environment affect my body as a messenger? The physical environment that my mother lived in at the time of my birth was less than ideal. My parents lived with my paternal grandparents who were viciously opposed to my parents' marriage. My father's background was Hindu and my mother's was Muslim: a definite taboo, even though they weren't in their respective homelands.

The belief was that these religions would not be able to peacefully co-exist and the marriage would be doomed from day one. I sometimes wonder if my parents should have married each other even though they were pregnant with their first child. It was considered a disgrace to impregnate a young girl, to take her honour, and then not marry her. I still wonder if my parents would have made different choices if they had had free will without the pressure of two cultures and religions to contend with. Ultimately, I think they would have made different choices and that some of the disconnection could have stopped a very long time ago.

As I reflect back to my early beginning, I wonder when the reality of my situation started to impact me. I have limited knowledge of my early years, and my memories are quite different from my older sibling. I believe one of my coping mechanisms was to weed out the bad and focus on the good. As I look at early family pictures, my smile was an undeniable grin up to the age of six or so. Did I block things out or did I not realize the magnitude of the issues in my family? Not everything was bad because I also have good memories of my childhood. My house was always full of people and I recall so much laughter and joy; these are the moments I seem to be able to draw on. Therefore, I'm unsure what I did with all the chaos and sadness.

At this early stage, according to the Sensorimotor Stage of development, what did I take in? Essentially, I believe that I took in information and beliefs about the world, others, and myself. At this primary stage, these are the core necessary things that each and every child expects from the primary caregiver.

As I reflect back on my son's primary needs, I wonder what this stage must have been like for me as a child. This is when a child starts to learn whether or not their primary needs are met. As I think about the beginning of my son's life I realize what an important responsibility a parent has to ensure that a child's needs are met. This is when parents learn about their child and the child learns to have its needs met by its parents. Within a short period of time, my son developed different kinds of cries in order to let us know what he needed, and as new parents we tended to his needs until we figured out exactly what he needed.

When I needed something, did I get the attention I needed, and what kind of attention was it? I often reflect on the times my own son woke up in the night and wondered if I was able to attend to his needs. Even though I had stressors during these times, they were nothing compared to the ones that my mother would have contended with and felt.

One of the stressors that occurred during my pregnancy was when my ex-husband was out until the wee hours of the morning with his friends. Again, the stress I was under must have been at a deep core level and my son may have felt it, but after he was born I tended to his every need each time he cried. I hope meeting his every need negated the extra cortisol he may have received at the stressful times during my pregnancy.

Just like my mother, my alarm bells were activated at an early age because of the traumatic environment I was born into. How did this impact my development and my life? Trauma turns on these alarm bells and once they are activated, they continue to stay on and are never quite turned off. In the limbic part of the brain where all sensory memory is stored, there is a part of the brain called the amygdala, which protects us. When we are in danger, whether real or imagined, our body decides whether to fight, flight, or freeze. This is when the brain constantly scans for threats and this impacts so many things. Our sense of rightness in the world becomes flawed as we begin our lives. Then, the body almost becomes an alien state—one of hyper-arousal. For example, when a young baby starts to scan his or her environment on an ongoing basis for anything that may impact safety, that child starts to disconnect from what he or she truly feels in their bodies. At such an early stage of development, young children start to protect themselves with the fight or flight response. According to Piaget in the Sensorimotor Stage of life, children learn through their senses that their environment is unsafe. Then, they start to protect themselves from real and minor threats, and end up in a space where they are not able to feel safe and relaxed.

If I started to respond to keep myself safe at such an early stage, what kind of basic developmental factors would I have missed as a young child? As a result of my need to protect myself, I started to ignore my thoughts, feelings, and body sensations. As a little girl, I really loved both my parents, but I wondered when the horrid abusive situation would end. I wanted my parents to get along. Sometimes they did get along. I always thought they would do their best for my siblings and me, but with time I realized that they were too caught up in their own world. So, as a young child, I needed comfort and caring, but instead I received uncertainty and instability. All six of us children huddled in one room where we shoved our heads in the pillows so that we couldn't hear what was going on. My older siblings tried to comfort us the best they could, but they also needed the care and comfort of their parents, who were embroiled in battle. They tried to take care of us younger ones by being brave, but really, how brave could they be when they were only a few years older than me?

Early on, my body became a war zone in which I fought off all the signs of trauma that I experienced. I became hypersensitive to each and every threat once my startle response was triggered. I missed out on all the good, joyful things in the world because

I needed to stay on guard in order to make sure that my world remained a safe one. As a child, I started to develop a real sense of sadness that these two people who loved us so much could not work out their issues long enough to take care of their own children. Subsequently, I learned to ignore my needs and I did not to ask for much in life because my parents' actions, or lack of them, taught me to believe that my needs were irrelevant. When I reflect back, I realize that my issues in life started quite young and that the external cues in my environment created internal messages in my body that left a lasting imprint on my life's blueprint.

At an early age, I tried to define the world through my surroundings, but the formulation of my worldview was skewed. I was not allowed to explore the world as a safe place. Instead, I learned that the primary people in my world were less than safe, so I couldn't take in all the wonder of the world without the veil of perpetual uncertainty. Basically, my environment shaped my internal views, and my internal views prevented me from feeling safe in my surroundings; this became a vicious circle of uncertainty.

I viewed the world as unsafe and uncertain, and people weren't to be trusted, so I had better be on guard. My senses were aroused whenever there was tension of any sort. My physiological cues were set off; my heart raced, my muscles went tense; my thoughts raced, and I suffered from hyper vigilance. I could not remain calm if I felt threatened. Whether this threat was real or imagined, it impacted my thoughts, feelings, and my internal emotional world. My body became something that protected me, but it also housed all the feelings of being raised in an uncertain world. Therefore, I started to disconnect from my body instead of understanding whether the threat was real or imagined so that I could manoeuvre through the world with less stress.

Check-In Questions

When you were a child, were there any circumstances that you may have been exposed to on an ongoing basis that impacted your place of safety?

Describe what you can remember about how you related to your early surroundings. Were you open to explore as your development dictated your curiosity?

Were your primary caregivers always there to support you emotionally, psychologically, physically, and spiritually as a young child?

How did you think about the world around you? How did you relate your internal space to the external world around you?

When you look back at your early family pictures, describe your moods in the pictures.

CHAPTER 8:
Developmental Paths from Childhood to Teen Years to Adulthood

As you reflect back on your life, I would like you to ask yourself if there were any issues in your primary life that might have impacted the particular developmental path that you took. In the following pages I will review the impact of trauma in my life from childhood, to teen years, to adulthood. I will review the following: personal, social, language, cognitive, and emotional development.

After each of the stages are defined through the behavioural and developmental areas, I will then analyze my own stages and how these stages impacted my life's blueprint. In reading a breakdown of my own life, I hope you can use my analysis of my developmental paths to help you understand your own developmental paths in life. After each section, there is space for you to write down your own blueprint and compare it to mine. We will first begin with childhood.

Childhood

Outlined below are the Guidelines of Normal, Personal, and Social Behaviour. There are three stages in childhood.

From birth to two years old

Attachment:

- Babies settle when their parents comfort them; respond to

their mother's eyes, voice, and face within a few hours of birth by giving signs to their mother that they want to be picked up or they may look away and need a break if they are receiving too much stimulation from their mother.

- Toddlers explore, knowing that they have a safe place to return to with their caregiver.
- Five months old: respond to social cues including facial expressions and gestures.
- Nine months old: socially interactive and plays games such as patty-cake with caregivers.
- Eleven months old: can develop stranger anxiety, separation anxiety, and practice solitary play.
- Two years old: will often play with others and imitate plays of others they see around them.

From four to six years old

Play:

- Cooperative with others.
- Imagines and develops stories and characters in play.
- Demonstrates reciprocation by taking turns in games.
- Develops motor skills and social skills.
- Experiments with social roles while playing.
- Reduces fears.
- Wants to please others.

From seven to eleven years old

At this age, friendships are specific to the child's situation.

- Starts to understand concepts of right and wrong.
- Relies upon rules to guide how they behave and play.
- Five to six years old: realize rules can be changed.
- Seven to eight years old: may be more reliant on rules.

- Nine to ten years old: rules can be negotiated; begin to understand social roles and can adapt behaviour to fit different roles and situations; takes on more responsibilities at home; and less fantasy play, but more team sports and board games.

My Blueprint Analysis:

Considering my mother's environment and circumstance, I'm unsure of whether my mother had the peace of mind to respond to some of my early needs. My mother's sadness may have also impeded my continual need for connection. I did not have the consistency and safety of the consistent facial reactions, vocal tones, and face of a mother who was present. This inhibited my ability to read to the necessary cues that I needed to develop a sense of security. Additionally, my bodily cues were inconsistent; therefore, I was unsure of what to expect. Most of the time, I was quiet when I was picked up.

Your Blueprint Analysis:

_____

_____

_____

_____

_____

_____

_____

My Blueprint Analysis:

With the chaos of three other younger children, I'm unsure if my mother was able to respond to my needs (such as being picked up in a consistent way) and as a result, I developed an attachment issue. My mother's availability to me became inconsistent because she had a difficult time due to abuse and caring for three other babies. As a result, I developed the internal knowledge that not all my needs were valid and that when I needed my mother, she was not always available. If a child doesn't learn how to soothe itself internally by learning from the reflective lens of the primary caregiver, then the child will typically develop an attachment disorder often referred to as separation anxiety. Attachment disorders occur when a child is not securely attached nor assured that all their needs will be met.

Your Blueprint Analysis:

_____

_____

_____

_____

_____

_____

_____

_____

_____

My Blueprint Analysis:
I went through years of separation anxiety, which manifested when I did not have my mother's undivided attention. These were much bigger issues than regular separation anxiety, since the nurturing of my needs was inconsistent. My anxiety was a lot higher, especially in relation to attachment issues, compared to a child who had their needs met on a consistent basis. As a child, it made sense that I was clingy, because I was unsure whether my mother would come back to me. I did not learn to self-soothe my needs. I loved others externally versus internally for comfort.
Your Blueprint Analysis:

My Blueprint Analysis:

The ability to learn to say "no" was difficult for me considering I was not sure whether I would be rejected or not. Being able to articulate my needs was difficult for me. It was also difficult to differentiate myself from my primary caregiver because I needed her ongoing and inconsistent support. So learning to differentiate from her would have brought too much anxiety. Ideally at this stage, separation should be a healthy thing to experience, but in my case, my times of separation brought too much distress. I was aware of the freedom I had to be in my own space from an early age, so I disconnected from my needs in order to be the kid whom others liked. I never made trouble as a kid, even if this meant giving others their way all the time.

Your Blueprint Analysis:

_____

_____

_____

_____

_____

_____

_____

_____

_____

_____

Ages and Stages and Language Development

Early on, my ability to question and vocalize was immediately impaired because of the fact that my freedom to vocalize was identifying my need and then verbalizing it in order to get that need met—which it often was not. Developmentally, our language evolves as we do; therefore, I question how my language was impacted by my circumstances and external environment.

As before, there are three stages in childhood. Outlined below are the Guidelines of Language and its influence on Behaviour at each particular stage.

From birth to two years old

Babies communicate their needs by vocalized cries, facial expressions, and body movements. Within the first months, different types of communication develop such as the following:

- Makes sounds.
- Laughter when curious or happy.
- Uses gestures to get attention.
- Imitates sounds.
- Increased verbal skills (up to ten words).
- Uses different sounds to get help when needed.
- Starts to understand verbal cues (both verbal and non-verbal).
- Becomes sensitive to its caregiver's tone of voice and body tension.
- Six months old: vocalization including crying, utterances, and playing language games.

From four to six years old

Communication:

- Increased understanding of vocabulary and concepts such as "yesterday" and "tomorrow," and can use these concepts in sentences.

- Demonstrates frustration when having difficult expressing themselves.
- Benefits from caregiver assisting with identifying feelings and ideas.
- Enjoys telling and listening to stories.
- Enjoys word games and may use objects to represent other things, and acts out scenes with others.

From seven to eleven years old

Communication:

- Uses language to anticipate the next event in a movie and draw conclusions about how situations may end.
- Uses long and intricate sentences.
- Understands other points of view and can form an opinion on whether they agree or disagree.
- Understands comparative sentence structures; for example, "it was earlier than yesterday."
- May start conversations with adults and children they don't know.

My Blueprint Analysis:
The freedom to use my voice was constricted at quite a young age. In our house, a baby's vocalization was not permitted. The imitations I learned were ones that I shouldn't have learned; for example, yelling and screaming. In a constricted way, I played language games with my family. I was allowed to babble, but the stress level of my environment (and whether my parents were getting along with each other) dictated my level of noise. Constriction of a child's voice leads to a lack of development of experimentation with that child's voice. Using the voice teaches the child a lot about themselves, others, and the world.

Your Blueprint Analysis:

_____

_____

_____

_____

_____

_____

_____

_____

_____

_____

My Blueprint Analysis:

In our house, vocalizing our intentions happened in a very haphazard way. The lack of language exposure meant that I could verbalize sometimes but not at other times. During these other times, verbalization was non-existent or was followed by harsh punishment. As a child, I was conditioned to limit my vocalization. Learning to listen to the slight deviations in rhythmic changes was difficult because I was always ready to protect myself against the slightest sign of threat. My alarm bell (or the amygdala—the part of the brain that stores threat) was developed, so any change meant a threat; as a result, my language abilities were limited. I needed to have a sense of openness to share my ideas and stories. I vocalized and shared at times, but at other times I was silenced. These language restrictions in a person's childhood result in them losing their voice symbolically, which I can relate to as I review my life.

Your Blueprint Analysis:

_____

_____

_____

_____

_____

_____

_____

_____

Outlined below are the Guidelines of Cognitive Development and its influence on the three stages in childhood:

From birth to two years old

The fetus can learn sounds and can respond to them after birth, so they think with their eyes, ears, and senses. They learn a lot about themselves and the world around them. At this stage newborns, cognitively develop in the following ways:

- Sucks to make certain visual displays and sounds.
- Increase in memory.
- Knows their body parts and may recognize familiar pictures.

My Blueprint Analysis:
I had a fair amount of freedom to explore sounds; however, my mother controlled and maintained peace in our environment by restricting this exploration when things were tense. If I did not explore openly, then the freedom to listen to my body would have been impacted. If I was quieted down along with three other children so peace could be maintained, then my ability to properly explore life was impaired. Therefore, I did not take in all the things I needed at this stage.
Your Blueprint Analysis:

_____

_____

_____

_____

_____

From four to six years old

A lot of cognitive learning also happens at this stage:

- Learns how to organize things in hierarchies.
- Pretends and makes believe.
- Thinks logically.
- Understands conversations of importance.

My Blueprint Analysis:
I took part in make believe and used my imagination; however, this was still constricted by my circumstances. I played a lot with my siblings and there was a lot of joy and laughter at this age.
Your Blueprint Analysis:

_____

_____

_____

_____

_____

_____

_____

_____

_____

_____

From seven to eleven years old

Cognitive learning:

- Seven to ten year olds: recognize when behaviour is intentional.
- Ten to eleven year olds: recognize and consider other points of view.

Concrete operations:

- Can accurately perceive events.
- Capable of organizing thoughts logically and rationally.
- Reflect upon self and attributes.
- Understands concepts of space, time, and dimension.
- Can remember events from months or years earlier.
- Effective coping mechanisms.
- Can understand how their behaviour affects others.
- Understands concepts of "right" and "wrong."
- Relies upon rules to guide behaviour and play because they provide the child with structure and security.
- Nine to ten years old: rules can be negotiated.
- Begins to understand social roles and regards them as inflexible.
- Can adapt behaviour to fit different situations.
- Capable of more responsibilities at home.
- Less fantasy play, but more team sports and board games.
- Compares one thing to another.
- Pays attention to small details.
- Understands the concept of beginnings, and that games can be played in different directions, such as backwards and forwards.

My Blueprint Analysis:

At this stage, finding clarity in my mind was difficult for me. Being able to focus enough to start to think logically was difficult for me because internally I was dealing with a lot of uncertainty. Since my external world was inconsistent, I had difficulty finding a balance between quieting my mind and manoeuvring through these necessary cognitive steps of development. At this point, I remember feeling overwhelmed with school. I had to work very hard on things that appeared so easy for my classmates to conquer. I constantly felt it was an effort to listen and concentrate in class, and if there were directions that were too lengthy in nature, then I disconnected from the lesson. I wasn't ever interested in games such as cards, checkers, or any game that involved logic because I couldn't follow the patterns for any extended period of time. I did well in school, but only because of the sheer effort that I put in to succeed.

Your Blueprint Analysis:

_____

_____

_____

_____

_____

_____

_____

_____

Emotional development is a major part of our childhood. In my blueprint, this is where most of the issues are because my inhibited emotional development eventually played out in my emotional relationships later in life.

Outlined below are the Guidelines of Emotional Development and its influence on the three stages in childhood:

From birth to two years old

The milestones of emotional development between these ages are numerous. Skills are developed include the following:

- Love can be demonstrated with physical affection.
- Fear caused by loud noises.
- The basic emotions begin to surface: shame, pride, envy, embarrassment, pleasure, excitement, joy, fear, anger, and sadness.
- Need caregivers to understand their feelings and respond to them with comfort and protection.
- Capable of socializing by smiling in an interaction.
- Responsive to the emotions of others.
- Begin to feel empathy and attachment to others.
- Increased autonomy.
- Affection and the need for a secure base.
- Develops emotional constructs of time and predictability.
- Feels safe with consistency.

From four to six years old

Emotional development:

- Says how they feel: sick, happy, or miserable.
- Strive for praise and acceptance.
- Express their feelings instead of repressing them.
- Demonstrates a sense of self-confidence in their knowledge of how things are done.

From seven to eleven years old

Emotional development:

- Capable of understanding principles behind rules.
- Capable of understanding rules and apply their own code of rules.
- May be aware of their own failures and shortcomings and be sensitive to their inabilities.
- Able to objectively view their own actions and motives.
- Ability to analyze failures and makes plans to change.
- They can understand most emotions and are capable of regulating their feelings, empathizing with others, and being aware of others' emotions.

My Blueprint Analysis:

At this point in my development, there were many times when I was allowed to feel, but my feelings were not necessarily allowed to evolve. My mother was always attentive, but my father was emotionally available only on his terms. He loved his children, but he wasn't patient or amenable to our needs. He interacted with us only when it suited him. It is important for children to learn to mimic their parent, but I did not have a free rein with my indulgent mother, who had emotional and physical constraints, or with my father, who could only display love in a sporadic way. By this point, I learned that I couldn't freely express my feelings, so the ability to use a myriad of ways to deal with my feelings wasn't in my repertoire. I was either non-expressive or over-the-top expressive—nowhere in between. I lacked the roles in my primary world to help me see the various effective ways of how to regulate my feelings. I did not use my words well when I was in highly triggered situations. I often vacillated from depressed to angry without much modulation of feelings in the middle. My ability to pull ways to effectively cope from my repertoire was vastly impaired at this stage of my development.

Your Blueprint Analysis:

_____

_____

_____

_____

_____

_____

_____

_____

_____

_____

_____

_____

_____

_____

_____

_____

_____

My Teenage Years

During the teenage period of my life, my sensors were developing for what I needed in order to securely attach to others in my world. My uncertainty taught me that I needed to create a space where safety and security were constant, which I began to do through the choices I made at quite a young age. As I planned the life that I wanted to develop for myself, I discovered that attachment to my parents was central in my blueprint. The environment my primary caregivers created for me impacted my life quite early on. I started to gain an understanding of my world and what it entailed.

In reference to theorist John Bowlby in his Attachment Theory, I see that my attachment type was an "Insecure Avoidant Attachment." Children in this type of attachment become more angry and clingy with their parents. Parents who are insecurely attached to their families aren't able to provide the same kind of consistency, care, and emotional responsiveness in comparison to securely attached parents.

At this stage of my life, I started to search for partners who did not make me feel insecure. I picked relationships where the boys were smitten with me and I felt that they would never leave me. I was rather clingy, but I didn't show this to my new partners. Instead, I pretended I didn't need them. I ended relationships even before the young men had any thoughts of dumping me. I didn't go too deep into relationships in my teenage years because I was too afraid of getting hurt. I also didn't allow myself to explore what I truly needed in relationships because as soon I thought there was a possibility of the relationship ending, so that I would be left alone, I ended things first. I never allowed myself the space to learn what I needed through consistency, emotional responsiveness, or through the genuine caring of a partner. I picked guys who were as clingy as I was, and who also brought with them the same type of attachment or some close variation of it. At this stage of my life I was hell bent on finding someone who wouldn't leave me. In the end, I missed some core learning opportunities at this early developmental stage.

Overall, safety and security were the lures of a relationship for me. I wanted someone to be so enamoured with me that I would finally have what I needed in my life. At this stage of my life I focused on other things such as academics and friendships, but most of my focus was on having a relationship, and this yearning continually kept me searching for my Mr. Right.

As I reflect back on this stage, there was one young man who was the healthiest choice for me, but I wasn't emotionally able to see it at the time. He came from a securely attached family system and he brought with him all the abilities to create a good life with me. I didn't realize this until years later. I was too busy trying to find security in all the erroneous qualities that I searched for.

I remember my first kiss. This is an indication of how much I needed things on my own terms. I remember wanting to kiss the young man who was the most stable, but this didn't happen, so I kissed someone else because I was angry with the stable young man. Instead of listening to what I was truly feeling, my need for security dominated my emotions. On the whole, this is a good example of how, if I had been able to listen to what was really good for me, I would have made healthier choices.

This pattern continued throughout my teenage years. I always picked young men who were perfect in the beginning, but in the end they abandoned me, leaving my heart broken yet again. I was adamant that I just needed to find the right boy, but I only picked the wrong boys. I carried on thinking that I just had to make better choices.

Could I see my role in the choices I was making? I was picking boys who were emotionally unavailable, inconsistent, and clingy. When I think back to the young men I had in my life, I realize there were a lot of great stable guys around me, but I needed to deal with my insecurities in order to start and keep a relationship with them. At this point in my life, I didn't have the introspective lens that surfaced as I grew emotionally.

This is where my attachment type impaired my ability to see the good qualities in the one young man whom I really cared for and still do, to this day. I realize he had all the qualities that I needed in a relationship at that time. In retrospect, I had always attracted emotionally healthy young men. However, I didn't have the knowledge or emotional intelligence to see the core essentials of a healthy emotional man because of my limited exposure at such a young age.

In your life, how did your upbringing impact how you became attached to others? Please review the following styles of attachment and see how or if they may have impacted some of the relationship choices that you may have made in your life that were less than ideal. This can include various intimate, work, or family relationships.

Secure Attachment:

Teens in this category have fewer issues with adjustment problems. These teens have a lot of consistency in their lives, and they are parented developmentally at an appropriate level throughout most of their lives. Overall, these teens receive the appropriate emotional responsiveness, consistency, and care.

Your Blueprint Analysis:

_____

_____

_____

_____

_____

Insecure Avoidant Attachment:

This type of teens can become obnoxious, clingy, or angry with their parents. Parents of this group come from the same type of family background, so they're unable to provide the things that their teens need for consistency, emotional responsiveness, and care.

Your Blueprint Analysis:

_____

_____

_____

_____

_____

_____

_____

_____

_____

_____

_____

_____

_____

Insecure Ambivalent Attachment:

These teens grow up with disorganized, neglectful, and inattentive parenting. These parents are not able to provide psychological strength after divorce or other major changes, and the child becomes clingy and inconsolable during times of distress. In general, these teens can suffer from mood swings and can become oversensitive to stress.

Your Blueprint Analysis:

_____

_____

_____

_____

_____

_____

_____

_____

_____

_____

Your attachment style is a very telling sign of the choices you may have made in the relationships you have made throughout your life. Some of these choices can be rectified if you realize that your choice of partner or work relationship needs to be adjusted or changed. The key here is your knowledge of the attachment style and understanding its impact on your life.

In my case, I walked ahead thinking I had found the perfect partner, and indeed things worked for a long time. Our styles of attachment worked for us throughout the ages of eighteen to thirty-five. In all fairness, this constituted a success relationship at this point in our lives because the real difficulties didn't show up until later adulthood. My insecure avoidant style worked well with his insecure ambivalent style. We were both able to give each other what we needed until the next stage of the game: adulthood and preparing for a family. This is when I started to ponder the life choices I had made at the tender age of eighteen. Until this point, I felt I had everything I needed in a marriage, that is, until I started to look for certain things in the next stage of my life that were glaringly non-existent. At this time, I stopped to evaluate what I needed by way of emotional responsiveness, consistency, and care.

My Twenties through Mid-Thirties

Prior to my twenties, I had not really questioned my life choices or reflected on them. However, the big questions I started to ponder came to light when my life started to shift. All the things I took for granted in my relationship appeared to be slowly slipping away from me. For the most part, I felt good about a lot of the things I had created in my life, but the one area that appeared to need some serious attention was my intimate relationship. I thought all of my hard work had been done around the area of relationships, but all the foundation blocks I had so clearly built for my life of safety and security were brought down in a major avalanche. Was I prepared? Hell no! The therapist within me said that I could handle this, but the emotional part of myself knew that it was bigger than I realized.

What is My Role in Life?

I remember thinking that life was supposed to flow. My upbringing was less than ideal, but I had built a pretty good life with a great partner. The next logical step was the legacy that we would leave behind. This was when I questioned our deviation of values. For years we worked together to build our careers, our home, and a financial life that was comfortable, so the next logical step in my mind was to start a family. Wasn't that what everyone wanted? Well, I was in for a rude awakening. We didn't have the right home, our finances needed to be bolstered, we needed to travel a little more, and we needed to be emotionally ready for the immense needs of supporting a child. I went along with my husband's checklist until I realized I couldn't wait too much longer because my biological clock was ticking. I had let my partner rationalize our decision to keep waiting, but I needed to verbalize my need so that he could clearly understand that we needed to make a decision. This is when I started to question whether my partner wanted the same things in life as I did but I thought we could surely get through this life stage after all this time we had spent building our lives together.

I also realized I had allowed my partner's perspective about this decision to be more important than my perspective. I needed to start asserting myself until the issue of creating our own family was on the table. My partner wouldn't relent on the decision to have a family. Consequently, I forced the issue, and for the first time in my life we entered a therapy office.

We always prided ourselves as a young couple that had the tools to resolve concerns, but this issue got the better of us so we needed someone who had an objective view to mediate the issue. It was tough to talk my partner into going to therapy with me, but we went and started the counselling process. Needless to say, we regressed well before we advanced in the process, and the discussions that came out of the sessions were very hard for me to process. Nonetheless, I realized I had ignored a lot of signs and the sessions showed me that my partner didn't want to have a family.

The signs that I ignored would have told me he was afraid of commitment. Was this because I didn't want to acknowledge these signs? Or, was I so hell bent on getting what I needed to create this image of my life that I had ignored the things he shared with me over the years? I ignored the signs because I knew he loved me and I always believed that our love would survive every challenge.

Here are some issues that developed in my blueprint due to a disrupted attachment that I should have been more aware of prior to the ensuing crisis:

1. Learning and reciprocating trust; using trust as a template for all future relationships. **Blueprint**: I learned that trust was really hard to find. I saw this from a very early age from my parent's relationship, my adolescent relationships, and from most family relationships that I was exposed to from an early age.
2. Exploration of environment with feelings of safety and security, which leads to healthy cognitive and social development. **Blueprint**: I learned that feeling safe wasn't consistent in my environment, so my cognitive (thinking) and social (relationships) development were impaired.
3. Developing the ability to self-regulate, which enables one to develop the ability to regulate impulse control and feelings. **Blueprint**: The ability to regulate and control my feelings wasn't something I could have done. I continually quieted them to maintain peace in my chaotic environment.
4. Creating a foundation based on an identity that includes a sense of competence, self-worth, and a balance between dependence and autonomy.

Blueprint: This formation of my identity was skewed. I didn't allow myself to understand who I was and what I needed to have in order to be whole in a relationship. I lost myself in relationships; I always hoped that love from my significant other would make me whole. I had an imbalance of dependency and autonomy. From the onset, the cornerstone of my relationships was dependency.

5. Generating a core belief system that included cognitive assessments of self, caregivers, others, and life in general. **Blueprint**: I wasn't allowed the space to really learn to listen to what I needed as a child, so this impacted my view of the world, other people, and myself. Subsequently, this worldview included a lack of safety and security.

6. Providing a defense against stress and trauma, which involves resourcefulness and resilience. **Blueprint**: I was born into stress; therefore, my resilience was limited. I wasn't devoid of trauma, so I also had a limited ability to develop resourcefulness.

When I look at the choices that I had made up to this point, I realize that I used all the resources from my environment to formulate my relationships. What were my true needs and desires for an enduring, caring relationship? I questioned the emotional connection I had in my relationship. I didn't factor in the other person's issues and how those issues might end up toppling the little bubble I had developed. Here I was, thirty-two years old, and my life was generally good, but soon my marriage would be dismantled because of the concerns that were a stage in a relationship's growth.

I ignored these messages, which should have been discussed throughout the relationship:

- He had a girlfriend when we met and he didn't end his relationship with her straight away.
- He continued relationships with both of us for a period of time.

- When he decided he wanted a relationship with me, he had difficulty breaking off the relationship with his girlfriend. Shockingly, he said they were considering ending their lives instead of dealing with the pain of him having to make this choice.
- As a teenager he hung out at strip clubs and had casual relationships with strippers.
- He took a survey in his first year of university and the professor shared with him that he was suffering from depression.
- He was obsessed with building his muscles to the point where he used steroids.
- We secretly got married and then he told his mother. He also asked me to keep my maiden name even after we were married.
- He had a lot of adverse feelings towards his mother: he treated her nicely to her face, but he expressed disdain towards her behind her back.
- He had strained relationships with his family.
- His best friend was too much a part of our lives. I thought it was closeness, but it was actually a fear of intimacy.
- He still maintained a single lifestyle, even after we were married; he went out with his single friends all the time.
- He did not put me, his wife, before his friends.
- He did not want to spend quality time at home; he was always bored with his life.
- His drinking increased.

Why did I ignore these issues at the early stage of the game? I had assumed that we were just settling down and that he would eventually change. Don't we all go through developmental life stages and eventually settle with time? This was not the case in my reality. My reality was that our worlds worked very well until the facts were revealed, and what we wanted wasn't the same any longer. My husband liked the lifestyle that we had created, and he didn't understand why I would want to give it all up to have a child. To him, my longing to have a child represented many things he didn't want to explore.

Did he love me? Yes, I believe he did, but no amount of love could get him to come to grips with the reality that his life was going to change and not by his choice. He could love me in limited terms, but loving a child would mean a deep kind of emotional attachment that he would never allow himself to feel again.

Nevertheless, we did have a child, and when he started to feel the loss of control and the feelings associated with real love, he abandoned both his son and me. He could deal with the pain on his own terms, but he couldn't deal with being left alone, which is exactly what he brought about in his life. His attachment issues ended our marriage. Did my past issues contribute? Yes they did, but what toppled our life together was his inability to regulate his feelings about his son.

I did my best to ignore my needs in our relationship, which scarred my trust, but my partner couldn't see how his own issues impacted his life. Due to his clouded judgment, he saw having our son as a deficit in our life and relationship—not an enhancement.

My own issues got in the way too because I accepted a reconciliation, which I shouldn't have done. I should have recognized that the issues at hand needed someone who had dealt with his issues of grief and who was willing to try all means necessary to make things better. Instead, I had someone who didn't want to take any responsibility to repair our marriage. Even though I appeared to be a slow learner, I tried to ensure I made the best choices for our newborn son. For four years, I held on to a situation that was already dead, and in the process, I felt myself getting lost. If I had quieted my mind and listened to and received all the messages that were around me, then I could have saved myself a whole lot of pain in the process.

I felt like I was failing my son if I gave up on my relationship with his father too soon. I know this is not a rational thought, but things became increasingly difficult. I had no choice but to heed the messages that I was given over and over again. My body did its best to alert me on a regular basis. I could not focus; I started to have massive allergic reactions. My face swelled up and I had to get two massive fibroids removed two years after the issues in my marriage ended, but I only listened when my life slowed down.

My life was filled, between my career, caring for a young child, and the chaos of managing a horrible marriage. I couldn't listen to my inner voice amongst all of this because the noise was too much to handle with all the clutter in my life. I started to slow my mind by sheer default. I felt like the universe was showing me the facts but I wasn't listening. However, the next sequence of events in my life brought me to a full stop. Ultimately, I needed to slow down, listen to my inner voice, and decide what was important to me. Inadvertently, it took a string of emotional traumas for me to realize this.

My first emotional trauma was in 2009 when I lost my job. I received severance pay in March 2010, and I left my marriage in July 2010. I didn't have a job or a plan. I was finally out of an abysmal situation; I had finally listened to my deep inner voice that said, "No more—time to go."

Slow Your Mind Down

"Slow your mind down" was something I always told my clients to do because the answers lay right beneath the surface. My own messages were there. I realize now that my fear of being alone had overshadowed having my courage to listen to that inner guidance. Slowing my mind was something I knew I should do intuitively as a child, but due to my family's circumstances I wasn't allowed to do it. However, even as an adult, I wasn't able to make this happen. I realized that I could talk the talk, but walking the walk was a whole different scenario.

Emotionally I was weak. I was meant to stay married; I took a vow—till death do us part. My vows were something I took very seriously and then I realized I was the only one who was taking them seriously. Perhaps some of my ignorance (when I didn't listen to the cues) was because I believed I could change anything if I set my mind to it at that time in my life. Again, I did not take into account that there was someone else involved—in this case, my husband—with distinctly different goals and no intention to keep our marriage together.

Listening to my inner voice allowed me to reconnect with my own values. I often think that it is phenomenal that we are born with sensory ability even while in the uterus. During my pregnancy, I realized how precious the space is for the beginning of a new life. It truly is a miracle. Having a child forced me to listen very closely to what I valued. I did not completely disconnect from the things I wanted, but I allowed my outside reality to inform my inside world. It's unfortunate that the elements in my childhood dictated that I learn to cope by being guarded and protected from my primary relationships and, in turn, my environment.

I believe that each and every person has the innate ability to live the fullest life possible, but sometimes life dictates that we take another path. My path was altered; I didn't realize that my childhood impacted me as much as it did. Early on, I realized that I needed stability in my life and I was the only one that could create this for myself; however, at that time I believed I had passed the test in most areas of my life except for my intimate relationships. I picked men who demonstrated certain qualities that pulled me in, but they did not withstand a long-term relationship. I was taking part in a process called re-enactment. I was trying to get the kind of nurturing, love, support, and consistency from those men that I didn't get from my dad, but I picked men who didn't have those qualities. It was like a project. I was going to prove that I was lovable enough to transform these men to develop these qualities, and I would not let myself be abandoned by them the way I had been by my father. Does this sound a bit surreal? Yes, it was, and even though I consciously recognized it, I still repeated the same destructive pattern over and over again.

Most of all, I needed a man to have charisma because this was one of the attractive traits that my dad had. I also wanted someone who completely doted on me. Intelligence, ambition, and family values were also key traits for him to have. Putting family first was something that I valued, but now as I reflect on my choice for a lifelong mate, I realize my partner's family values were unfounded even though he came from a relatively good family.

I started to re-align with my values well into adulthood. When I was in relationships, I did have concerns. I said things such as, "He does not care about me." "He is self-centred." "Why is what I need not being taken into consideration?" I heard a lot of those messages in past relationships, or I felt the discomfort in my body when I was being treated badly, but I often told myself to stop being so rigid and to just go with the flow. I ignored those messages at the earlier stages of my relationship over and over again until the breakdown of my marriage in my thirties.

Now it is time for you to answer some questions for yourself. For example, when you look at your life, are you practicing your values by living them in your daily life? Are you living within your value? And if so, how do you know? If you are living outside of your values, then what areas of your body tell you that you are living outside your values? How do you know that you are living your values, in the core of your being?

This was a time of uncertainty for all but especially our child. He went from a place of two parents, to one parent, and then to a place where everything had changed. Even though things were tough during the last of years of the marriage, I did my best to shield my son from all the uncertainty that plagued my marriage and, in turn, his life.

During the two years of separation from my husband, I tried to continually reinforce to our son that we focus on the people we love when things are tough. My ex-husband demonstrated the opposite of this when he introduced our son to his girlfriend right after I left. My ex only focused on his own needs, so I did everything I could to ensure that my son saw a connection on my end. I spent all of my time off with him, and I tried to explain that even though we were going through a difficult time, we would get through it.

My ex-husband spent less and less quality time with our son, so I tried to fill in the gaps. Every time his father let him down, I surrounded him with people who cared about him and who would spend quality time with him. We went on vacations with my family and we spent lots of quality time together. We snuggled up to read and watch movies. Whenever there was a new issue with my ex, I discussed the situation openly with my son and reassured him that we could always discuss things and there was nothing that he couldn't say or that I couldn't handle. In time, my son learned to understand that staying connected during tough times is the richest gift of all.

Check-In Questions

Are there qualities that you used as a frame to pick your current partner that no longer fit your current frame of needs?

Can you define what health should look like in your relationships?

How did you learn about what you consider to be healthy?

Are your relationships, in fact, healthy and good for you in your current life?

What are your core beliefs and assumptions about a healthy relationship? Are they aligned with what you value?

If you are in a good relationship but there are difficulties, what methods do your use to address the concerns?

What are some of the constructive methods that you utilize and some of the less than constructive ones?

Where did these methods of resolution originate?

Describe your parents' relationship in detail.
What were the core elements of their relationship?

How did they demonstrate affection, deal with conflict, and negotiate change?

Describe a couple that you know who have a healthy relationship. Outline all the elements of their relationship that you consider to be healthy for their well-being and needs.

CHAPTER 9:
Case Studies

There are so many people who wade through life trying their best to create a life that fits the mould of their ideal. Perhaps these following case studies will give you a sense of what may be impacting your life and encourage you to think about issues that you haven't stopped to consider yet. Overall, I hope the window into the lives of these four people will give you an opportunity to see how their blueprints have evolved.

Case Study One: Early Abandonment

Early Childhood

This client was born out of wedlock as the result of an affair his father had with his best friend's wife. In his traditional culture, this child was born into a world of disgrace. His mother gave birth to him after her husband found out she had the affair; her husband then left her to raise their young daughter and her newborn son by herself. There was a lot of pressure put on her to abort the child but she kept him and, instead of putting him up for adoption, he was raised by his biological grandparents. However, his biological father wouldn't take responsibility for him, so his grandparents did their best to raise their grandchild on their low income. In essence, this young baby was brought into the world as an orphan without the love or support of either biological parent. Even though his grandparents took the responsibility to raise him, he always felt like he wasn't wanted and this belief was reinforced by many people in his life besides his parents.

His grandparents did their best to buffer him from the brutal comments and behaviours of others, but this young man's legacy was solidified quite early. He was consistently teased at school about the fact that he lived with his grandparents and he was also teased by his extended family; in fact, his male cousins often referred to him as the "bastard" child. At school, even though he was bright, his grandparents wouldn't get him involved in extracurricular activities and they were glaringly absent from school events. This young child was alone and sad. Therefore, he focused on what he could do well, which was academics. He realized early on that when he did well in school, he received praise from not only his family, but also from his teachers and others in the community.

The young boy spent a lot of time with his cousins, and at times this was a love-hate relationship; even though they loved him, they bullied him because his grandparents treated him differently from all the other grandchildren. In essence, his home—the place where he received the most support and love—also proved to be a weapon for his cousins to use against him. However, he developed a close bond with one set of his cousins to the point where he became a part of their family. The uncle of this family became a pivotal influence in his life, but unfortunately there was violence and infidelity in this family system as well.

Quite early on, this young man learned that he couldn't listen to what he needed on an emotional level, and this impacted the sequence of events that eventually led him to see a therapist. During this stage of his life, he never saw his mother and had only one or two periodic visits from his father, who at that time was studying abroad. The connection to his biological parents was almost non-existent.

Teenage Years

The client realized that girls and relationships were quite complicated. He was a good-looking young man, but he appeared to pick girls who weren't nice to him. He came off as secure and independent, but the girls he chose were as insecure as he really was. In his early female relationships, he developed but he did not have a separate sense of who he was. He became an extension of his girlfriends, instead of a person separate from his girlfriend. Even though he was sweet and caring to his girlfriends, he appeared to stifle them, and then they eventually broke off their relationships with him. When things didn't go his way, he became emotionally abusive. He didn't give his girlfriends space and when they asked for it, he would freak out because he was unable to control his feelings. He had few relationships throughout this stage, but he mostly walked away believing that he couldn't trust women, which enforced his belief that he was unlovable.

His grandparents continued to offer him love and support through this trying period of his life. His father started to visit him a bit more often. He knew his mother was alive and that she had moved away with his half-sister, but this was the only information he had about her. He openly shared that he hated both of them and he acted like he didn't care about them at all. Periodically, his father brought him presents, which he begrudgingly accepted because they financially helped his grandparents, who had used their limited resources to raise him.

The few interactions he had with his father made him feel even worse about his situation. When his father came to see him, it stirred up a lot of intense emotion in the young man. However, my client wouldn't invest in a relationship with his father because felt like he was a burden to his father and his father could only muster up a limited period of time to see him.

As the young man went through this stage, he focused on his schooling and his grandmother often reminded him, "With an education you'll be become somebody."

Those words stayed with him in his deepest and darkest times, but he always thought, "When I become someone, then I will be loved."

He took his grandmother's words seriously because they appeared to get him closer to what he wanted: connection.

After he finished high school, he left his grandparents' home and had to find another place to live because his father wouldn't take him in. He bounced around from various family members' homes until he could go abroad to attend university. Unlike all his other classmates, the young man couldn't afford to study abroad but shockingly, for the first time in his life, his father assisted him by funding his airfare to go overseas. There, he had to figure out how to pay for his university education on his own. Because of this opportunity, he went abroad and started working to put himself through school, and he did exactly, putting himself through undergraduate school and medical school. However, during that time he met a young girl and married her.

Early Twenties

He returned home within a week of his marriage. It had shocked everyone who was close to him. He barely knew this girl. They thought he had rashly jumped into marriage. Just as he had during his teenage years, he had picked another girl who had low self-esteem. This is when the real chaos began in his life. He had jumped into this marriage, and once again, he had chosen someone who couldn't be available to him in the ways that he needed her to be. She was also from a dysfunctional family. Plus, she was in a new country without any family connections. On the whole, she needed her new husband to support her as a new wife and mother. She needed him to be emotionally available to her but this became a problem because his emotions were shut down from his troubled upbringing. He could not meet her needs because he had needs himself that remained unmet, because they had not been addressed during his upbringing.

He wanted to feel that someone loved him and could be there for him regardless of his flaws; however, his new wife also had issues that she couldn't ignore. She needed support with the new baby and help getting used to a new culture, but he was too busy with work. Their life situation started to deteriorate quickly. As she stood up for her needs, my client became more and more insecure to the point where he became verbally and physically abusive to her. Nevertheless, they both stayed in the marriage. He focused on finishing school and starting his career because he was working to become the best physician possible; this meant that his hours were long and the amount of time that he spent away from his wife and son increased.

His connection to his biological parents became more frequent because he had more contact with them, but they did not increase the support that they gave him. His father had re-married and had a new family, so he was consumed with them as well as his business. My client really wanted support from his dad, especially as he began to crumble in his role of new father and husband. However, it was apparent that their father-son relationship would continue to be minimal. Nevertheless, my client still stayed connected to his father in any small way that he could.

My client's mother also re-connected with him, but she also maintained her distance. They got together and she asked him to take occasional trips with her, but my client always felt a distance from her. He maintained a connection with her out of the obligation that she was his mother. At this stage, his life became murkier and he recognized that his marriage was in a bad place. However, the worst moment in his marriage was when his wife stabbed him and he had to be rushed to the hospital. Their lack of ability to make a decision had caught up with them, and once again he was on his own. His wife and son left immediately, returning to her home country and her parents. My client followed so he could maintain a connection with his son, but this ultimately turned into a vicious custody battle with his wife.

The next year or so was the worst time of his life. He worked a lot to maintain his sanity and he entered counselling, but he found the process difficult due to all the pain that he was experiencing. The icing on the cake was when his wife took their son abroad, and my client didn't know where his son was for almost a year. The one thing that the client was most afraid of had occurred. His wife had abandoned him, and taken his son with her, which triggered the deep wound of his early abandonment by his parents. He knew he had to do something different with his life, but he couldn't see past his pain to recognize that these dark moments were teaching moments and they were showing him how he could move on with his life. My client spent a couple of years on his own and then he started to work on his own blueprint of life.

Thirty-Five Plus

When this client entered my office, he was distraught, angry, and bewildered with his life, but he also acknowledged that he wanted to live life to its fullest. Here he was, forty years old, and he had suffered abandonment by both his parents and his wife. He said the pain was too much to bear. It took almost five sessions before he was able to trust me. The significant people in his life had proven over and over again that they couldn't be trusted, so he struggled to allow me to enter a space where I could actually help him.

Once he was able to open up, he started to share how his childhood abandonment had affected him. He talked about how he felt that he wasn't worthy of love and how he repelled the people who really loved him: his grandparents, aunts, uncles, and cousins. He truly believed he was inherently flawed and that was why his parents had both abandoned him. Because of this belief, he disconnected from what he needed to do to evolve into the person he was meant to be. He had learned that listening to what was outside of him was more important than what was inside of him. He talked about feeling little of himself, and he told me that if someone did treat him nicely, then he would automatically let him or her into his life.

He perceived the women he dated as loving because they

actually paid attention to him. In his mind, that meant they really cared for him and then he would fall madly in love with them. When he turned off his inner voice, he negated what he was thinking, feeling, and needing. He based his choices and on the attention the other person was showing him, hence, his rash choices in relationships.

He had never allowed himself to feel the pain of his past. He felt that if he allowed himself to feel it, then it would consume him and he wouldn't be able to come out of it. We discussed the normalcy of emotions and the need to allow them the space to be validated. In cutting himself off from his feelings, he was in fact encouraging his pervasive belief that he was unworthy of love and this acted as an unconscious plane for all of his relationships. He needed to validate that emotional part of himself and to allow that part to be soothed so that he could listen to his inner voice telling him what he needed and wanted in a healthy normal relationship. At a young age, he wasn't allowed the space to just be where he could learn the skills of listening to his inner voice or a space where he could develop a sense of safety and security. Without space, he made black and white decisions, but eventually he did develop the capacity to see the grey area.

If someone deviated from his template, where they could love him unconditionally, then he automatically cut them off. However, if he had been allowed the space to develop his sense of self as a child, then he would have recognized that the other person in the relationship also had reciprocal needs. In his relationship with his wife, he was unable to understand her needs because his needs were all consuming. We discussed how, if he could provide the warmth and caring that he hadn't received from his parents to himself, he would then be able to meet his own emotional needs and, in turn, be able to develop the capacity to regulate his feelings in his future relationships. This concept was hard for him to grasp, but as he worked through the process he started to get a sense of how the unconscious platform from his early abandonment might have impacted his ability to truly connect with others. When my client reflected on all the connections in his life, he realized what he needed to do. We reviewed the patterns of his relationships from the past, then we focused on what he liked in those relationships, and then we finally determined what elements negated what he wanted most: connection.

Eventually, my client got over his upbringing and he focused on the value of what he gained from his extended family. The next difficult topic we tackled was the physical abuse his ex-wife inflicted and how this was the necessary paradigm shift he needed to gain connectivity with others. He recognized that when he could identify what his healthy normal needs were in a relationship, he could then figure out how to relate to potential mates in the future.

At first, these sessions were very difficult, but with time he recognized that he could control the choices he made in his relationships, and this became the turning point in his therapy. One of his major realizations was the fact that he might never have a real connection with his biological parents, who not only appeared to be incapable of meeting his emotional needs, but also the emotional needs of their grandson. As he grieved this loss, he was able to be really clear in recognizing that the life he was creating was based on what was important to him—not what he was born into.

The prognosis for my client was good, and with time he was able to take his life lessons from his blueprint forward in his life. After being single for a couple of years, he met a lovely woman who appeared to meet all the healthy emotional needs he was looking for in a long-term partner. After dating for a while, eventually he got married again (which was difficult for him) and several years later they had three fantastic children. The blueprint analysis of his life really enabled him to look at his life choices on a deep unconscious level.

After going through this process with my clients, I often wonder if they can take their new wisdom and make changes to create the life they want. In this case, I asked my client if he would be willing to share what he had learned and he consented.

Here are my client's own words about what this process was like for him:

"Sometimes I look around at my life and feel I have to pinch myself to see that in fact it's real. The process of looking at my life took a lot of strength that I didn't know I had. However, this was the best gift that I could have given myself. I would have lived a life of chasing connections and following my biological legacy to my grave. Today I feel in control of all my choices and I have gained a skill that I use continually. I have shared this skill with my first son and will do the same with the younger two girls. Out of my early trauma came a gift of introspection, which has allowed me to live the greatest life possible."

As you reflect on his life story, consider whether or not there have there been any issues early on in your life that may still resonate with you and hold you back from having connections with others. When we are abandoned early on in life, this can lead us down a path of destructive patterns.

I will now ask you some reflective questions on early attachment:

Check-In Questions

Did your early primary caregivers offer you a space to develop your own sense of safety and security?

How were you allowed to gain a sense of self at an early age?

Review your connections in your present emotional relationships. Are they the way you would like them to be?

Outline all the core needs that you require to exist in a healthy satisfying relationship.

In your present emotional relationship, are the emotional needs that you outlined for the above question being met?

If your emotional needs aren't being met, what steps do you need to take to ensure things are on track with your partner?

If you are in an emotionally unsatisfying relationship, why are you staying in it? Is this based on old messages from your parents, society, or other external factors?

Was there any abuse in your early relationships? And if so, how have these abusive experiences impacted your relationships throughout your life?

Case Study Two: Emotional Abuse

Sometimes we can't perceive or understand the concerns that cause couples to separate. This second case study is about a fifty-three-year-old woman who felt blindsided when, after thirty years of marriage, her husband asked for a divorce. She felt duped when he left her. After her separation from him, she discovered that she was repeating the same patterns in her following relationships; therefore, she decided to make changes in her life. When I met her, she had been separated from her husband for over ten years, but she recognized that if she didn't change the patterns within her relationships, then it might prove difficult for her to find a partner to spend the rest of her life with.

Early Childhood

This client grew up in a middle-class environment that was relatively devoid of turmoil. She grew up in a family of six where her father was the breadwinner and her mother was the stay-at-home mom. Their lives were pretty traditional with traditional values. She and her siblings all went to university and created middle-class lives for themselves.

As modelled by her mother, she grew up to be the perfect homemaker and she was available to meet her children's needs at all times. Her view of being a wife and mother was clearly defined, except she established herself as a professional, which was something that her mother hadn't done. Her father cared for his children but, in retrospect, he was not emotionally available to them. He was essentially a traditional male, and along with that came his belief that women were less dominant than their male counterparts.

She felt implications from an early age that she wasn't ever good enough in her father's eyes. She didn't feel good about herself and, in turn, this affected her self-image as a little girl. The path of this messaging wasn't obvious at this young age, but as my client started to discuss her early childhood memories she spoke of her father calling her names because her physical appearance did not meet his standards. Obviously, this was something she internalized quite young as part of her sense of self.

Teenage Years

My client appeared to enjoy the teenage stage of her life, but she consistently appeared to pick guys who didn't make her feel good about herself. She thought nothing of this and ploughed through her teens, and then at eighteen years of age she eventually met her husband, who appeared to be nice enough. They didn't date a lot, but she realized this young man was mild natured and he didn't talk too much. She was in love with him, and he with her, so they did the next logical thing and got married to each other.

In her mind, she was following the path of setting up a good life for herself with this mild-natured young man. During this period of her life, she was clear about her path; she wanted to finish her schooling and then proceed to the next logical step (as per her society's values), which was to have children. To her, this was simply logical and she followed what she thought was expected of her.

She loved her profession and felt good about her career choice. She received validation in her field, and this part of her life built up her self-esteem; meanwhile, other areas of her life seemed to wane at times. Deep down inside she didn't feel the best about herself; nonetheless, she still felt she had a great life: one that others would envy. As a young couple, my client and her husband experienced the same financial struggles as many other people do. They also weren't as passionately in love as they should have been, but they were satisfied with the life they had created for themselves. So, she tucked away any concerns she had about herself because her life was progressing quite well at this stage.

Early Twenties

This stage was progressing as per usual, but just like most couples, her intimacy with her husband was waning. By their mid-twenties, they had two beautiful children but my client saw she wasn't at the forefront of her husband's mind. Not only did my client feel that her husband was distant, but he also didn't appear to be paying much attention to her. As well, she was their children's primary caregiver; his parenting skills were non-existent at best.

Her husband appeared to be in his own world. This became most apparent when he changed careers and got a lot of attention from others in his professional field. At that time, the cracks in their marriage became more evident. Here my client was ten years into her marriage and, based on past messages she had received from her dad at a very young age, she now felt that she wasn't good enough for her husband either. There wasn't any conflict, but there wasn't any emotional intimacy either. She plugged along, believing that things would get better, and ignoring all the telltale signs that were glaringly obvious in front of her. She put her nose to the grindstone and focused on her professional career, becoming one of the best in her field, and excelling to the highest level possible all the while trying to ignore the other parts of her life that were beckoning for her attention. Inevitably, her husband not only ignored her more and more, but he also became more absent in his role as a father.

Chapter 9

Thirty-Five Plus

This is when this client's life appeared to begin to fall apart. Her kids were growing up and things were going well, but again, it was glaringly obvious that she was alone in her role as parent. She did everything related to her children from their educational needs to assisting with their extracurricular activities. She realized that after twenty years, her marriage was in trouble. She tried to approach her husband, who was living as a married man but only from a technical standpoint, because in reality he seemed to be living alone with three other people. Not only did his wife feel distant from him, but so did his children.

My client tried to see what could be done to resolve the situation. However, at this point she realized her husband's comments were the same as her father's: she wasn't good enough, she wasn't pretty enough, and then came the heart-wrenching realization that her husband was having an affair. One day, right after supper, she received a call from a strange woman asking for her husband. At first she told the caller that he wasn't at home and she didn't take a message from the woman. However, as she began to ruminate on the call, she realized there must be something going on. In the end, she called the woman back and the woman shared that she had been having an affair with her husband for the past two years.

My client was devastated by this news. She was aware that things weren't going well, but this was unconceivable. She waited until her husband finished his shift and arrived home. Then, for first time in their marriage, they had a frank discussion about all their problems. My client realized that her husband was unwilling to take responsibility for his part in the marriage. From his perspective, his new career had given him a lot of attention and he started to enjoy the attention he was getting from other women, especially his mistress. As a result, he started to treat his wife badly, just as her father had done to her.

My client chose to stay in the marriage, believing that they would try to work on it, but the infidelity didn't stop. Finally, my client decided to leave the marriage. She was distraught that her marriage was over. Emotionally, she reeled; she grieved. When my client entered counselling, she had never spoken to anyone about her concerns. Her friends and family had generally consoled her each time she had another failed relationship, but they did not see the overall picture. Therefore, they could not offer her the support she needed. This client's self-esteem was quite low. She had always believed the negative messages she'd received from a very young age. Even though she excelled at her profession, these negative messages started early and continued to play over and over in her head to the point that her actions were in line with her thoughts.

She eventually started to date again, but each new relationship appeared to have the same frame attached to them. They were all the "bad boys"—the ones who wouldn't commit. She liked the attention she received from these relationships, but she wanted a relationship where the dynamic was different. Still, she continued to instinctively pick men who cheated on her and, in turn, made her feel worthless. The men she dated were players, and she became the ideal person to be taken advantage of. Of course, she could not see this; instead, she saw her involvement with these men as passionate. She didn't see that they were players because she thought so little of herself. She perceived their attention as caring, but it wasn't. She was actually being used to fulfil these men's needs and nothing else.

In reviewing these relationships and being open about her thoughts, feelings, and behaviours, the client was able to see how she was selling herself short. At first she stated that she had made great choices in men, but when she started to analyze her role in these scenarios, she recognized that she allowed these men to treat her like an object, even though that was not her intention. She wanted a man to treat her with dignity and respect, but she had received the complete opposite. Finally, she recognized her poor choices and wanted to understand her role in the process.

She started to evaluate her upbringing and how she had allowed her father's negative messages to become a central theme in how she saw herself throughout her life.

For the most part, she felt unworthy of a healthy relationship. Deep down inside, she didn't feel she had what men wanted because she wasn't pretty enough. This client worked hard to recognize how that inner emotional part of herself was negated to the point where she attracted these scenarios into her life.

In order to get her life back on track, she needed to work on a series of steps. Her first order of business was to reconnect with the inner part of herself that received all these negative messages, and then clear them out and replace them with kinder, caring messages that would allow her to nurture herself. This exercise was tough, but she persisted at it and eventually she changed her negative paradigm to a positive one.

Eventually, she was able to start listening to her inner voice (the keeper of all values, beliefs, and assumptions), which was in line with the positive life she wanted. At times during the process, she felt she wasn't good enough for anyone, nor did not feel worthy of a good life, which didn't help her to make the necessary choices. However, in time, she could internally regulate her feelings and control her impulsive actions around the men who weren't good for her.

Slowly, she started to take care of the emotional part of herself, which translated itself outwardly in the way she dressed, and her self-confidence showed by the way she engaged with others. She made better dietary choices and started exercising again, which created a ripple effect; she felt better physically. Although she had lost weight in the past when it was an external directive, this time it was an internal one. She started to recognize her lack of self-esteem as an erroneous part of her that she really despised. On the whole, she wanted to be loved for who she was: a lovely woman with an excellent sense of humour who had a lot to offer.

When she learned the skills to slow her mind down, she realized the huge role she had played in perpetuating her situation.

She also realigned her relationship with her father and let him understand that she needed a different relationship with him. This was a difficult conversation for her to have; we role-played the conversation she would have various times during our sessions. She told him she needed kind positive feedback from him, and if he was incapable of this, then she would limit her interaction with him. Her father was a domineering, opinionated man, but smart enough to listen to what his adult daughter needed from him in order to maintain their relationship.

At present, my client continues to be single, but when she dates she is clear on what she needs in a relationship. If she sees any signs that he doesn't have the qualities she needs, then she is able to disconnect with relative ease. She feels a lot better about herself and doesn't feel the mad rush to fill her life with a man who would cause emotional scarring. She continues to enjoy her career, her adult children, and she is also involved in activities that foster the positive self-esteem she developed.

I will now ask you some reflective questions on early attachment:

Check-In Questions

How did you pick the emotional relationship that you are presently in?

When do you think of your formulation of sense of self? What were the early messages regarding your self? Were they positive or negative?

If you were to rate your self-esteem between one and ten, where would you fall? What needs to happen for you to have ideal self-esteem?

When you think of your own early childhood messages, are there any that held you back in life? If so, what are these messages?

What can you do to decrease or get rid of them altogether?

What are the qualities of your ideal emotional relationship?

Do you presently have these qualities in your present relationship? If not, why?

Case Study Three: Substance Abuse

This client is a forty-five-year-old woman born into a traditional upper middle class family. Due to her issues with drugs and alcohol, she decided to attend counselling. Her family upbringing was relatively good, except her parents didn't have a good marriage. Her family loved her, but she was shy. She had struggled with substance abuse since her mid-twenties, but she hid this from her immediate family.

Early Childhood

This young woman has six siblings; she is the second to last child. Her parents were hard-working people; her father was the breadwinner and her mother was the traditional stay-at-home mom. Her father was an entrepreneur, so he worked hard to take of his children and wife. The family was full of life and laughter, and her parents and older siblings cared her for. She was a very shy child who allowed her older siblings to speak for her. She was the child who hid behind her mother's legs when she went out in public.

My client stayed at home with her mother until the age of three and then she started nursery school. On the whole, the separation from her mother was difficult for her. Her mother spent more time with her than she did with her other children even though her time was divided between her seven children. My client was not able to feel secure within herself, so she felt distressed and could not soothe herself very well. She was a very anxious child and had difficulty feeling secure. This anxiety engulfed her and she spent a lot of time trying to manage her emotions throughout her life, which impacted her self-esteem and her ability to connect with others.

Teenage Years

The formative years of this young woman's life were relatively normal. Even though she was very shy and she was not one of the most popular girls, she was well liked and bonded with her friends. Academically, she did well in school, but not as well as her older sister. At an early age, she felt inferior to her sister, but this didn't appear to be an issue that would cause future problems.

She was like any typical teenager and she did a lot of developmentally appropriate things that most teens do. Early on, she got a part-time job at a card store. This life experience was more about social interaction than earning an actual paycheck.

Her first incident with alcohol was when she was fifteen years old. She attended a staff party and she was intoxicated when her mother came to pick her up. Her mother didn't make a big deal out of it because she associated it with being a normal teenager. After this incident, life resumed its normal flow.

Through her teenage years, she witnessed family violence; there was a lot of uncertainty and chaos in her family. Unfortunately, she and her siblings had the devastating burden of dealing with their family's uncertainty on a weekly basis. Throughout her teens, her drinking didn't appear to be an issue even when she started to date. Her parents didn't have any concern about her drinking either.

The next issue for her was relationships. She seemed to always pick boys who were well below her calibre and these boys consistently let her down. For example, she has a vivid memory of being stood up for a Sunday luncheon that she had planned with a boy. She also recalls thinking that she wasn't good enough and she felt very alone. She believed that no one would ever love her for who she was: a quiet, shy, caring, and vulnerable girl. She continued dating and was devastatingly hurt by each and every relationship.

Early Twenties

Her first major relationship was a major heartbreak. This relationship was with a young man who was a couple of years older than her. This was her first sexual experience and she felt truly in love. Months after their intimacy, he broke up without any explanation. Afterwards, she plodded along from her heartbreak and, in time, she started to date again. At this time, she met another nice young man.

Again, she was smitten, and she thought, *"This is the one."*

This man appeared to be everything she wanted. He was a decent young man, he came from a nice family, and she thought he was definitely ready for marriage. Then, out of nowhere, he broke up with her. She took a couple of years to recover from her break up with him, and even today she feels as though she's never fully recovered from this relationship.

In her own words, she had given up on being happy at this point in her life. She felt as though happiness wasn't ever going to happen to her. She said she looked around in her life and realized that not only did her parents have an unhappy marriage, but many others in her community shared the same fate. She truly believed that having a healthy relationship was like winning a lottery. So instead, she focused on her career as an artist. She received so much gratification from her work that it really took her focus away from relationships.

It was at this point in her life that her husband came along. They met at work. He was a lot older than she and full of flattery. He complimented her and showered her with all the kind words she had needed to hear for so many years. Within a short period of time they became involved and for the first time in her life, she felt as though her world was complete. They had a whirlwind romance and she moved in with him in spite of her family's opinion. They felt he was misrepresenting himself, but she didn't care. What did they know? She had finally found the man that would make her feel complete; her knight in shining armour had finally arrived.

She moved in with this man and the more involved she got with him, the less involved her family was with her. Each and every month she became more distant from them. She told her family how phenomenal he was, but in doing so, she distanced herself from the people who loved her. She assured them that life was great. She stopped attending most of her family's events, but when she did go, she would go alone without her new partner. When she was asked where he was, she said he was tremendously busy with his sales position.

Thirty-Five Plus

The chaos she was experiencing with her husband was even more horrible than the family thought. She had two children with this man. Due to the years of the distance between her and her family, she easily hid the signs of physical abuse. There was one incident when he hit her with a telephone; however, she told her parents it was her young toddler who had hit her. Her family accepted this explanation, but with much skepticism. She kept the years of abuse a secret from her family because she was too embarrassed to let them know that they had been right about their concerns. On top of being physically abusive, he was also an alcoholic and drug addict.

After years of abuse she finally left the relationship, but went right into the arms of a married man. She deflected what was going on within and started another relationship. She so happy in spite of the choice she made to be with a married man. Her family relished the change. They were happy she and her children were involved in their lives again, although years of separation seemed to have changed her.

Her ex-husband told her family that they should be concerned about her substance abuse, but that fell on deaf ears. However, as the years progressed, her substance abuse became more evident. In order for her to cope with her stress, she started drinking and dabbling with marijuana, which slowly developed into an alcohol and drug addiction. She fell further into substance abuse as the years went on. When her children were removed from her care, she sought help. The start of this client's counselling was less than smooth.

In her immediate family, there were no concerns with drugs or alcohol. However, on her maternal side of the family both grandparents were alcoholics and, in his earlier years, her father was dependent on alcohol. For her, these dependency issues didn't start to develop until she was in a relationship with her common-law husband. She shared that it was tough to be with him. She wanted to have a family. Very early in the relationship, she ignored his emotional abuse. However, well into her relationship, he started to physically abuse her, and her only escape was alcohol.

She loved her children, but recognized that she was incapable of taking care of them because she used alcohol to cope. She talked with me at length about her upbringing and discussed the role of alcohol in her culture; it was for socializing and not to be abused. Her father partied with her friends, but he misused alcohol.

She struggled with alcohol and drugs for years. It was her respite. When the phone was taken away because she didn't pay the bill, she had no connection to the outside world, so her two constants were drugs and alcohol.

She didn't think much of her own life, but she wanted a better life for her children. She loved her children too much to let this destroy their lives. After months of counselling, she finally attended inpatient treatment for her substance abuse. She continued with her counselling and, as she worked through her issues, she recognized there was a predisposition for addictions in her family, but her particular development of concern was situational.

She shared with me that as a young child she had some anxiety. She always felt worried and her worry increased when she realized that there were real issues in her family. As a child, she remembered being in class and not being able to focus. As an adult, she realized this was due to a combination of anxiety and early exposure to violence in her family. The issues with boys in her life came next.

Through her years of therapy and remaining focused on recovery, she recognized that her addiction had developed due to her life circumstances. She realized that her anxiety had a relationship with addictions. She tried to feel level instead of feeling so anxious all the time. All the detrimental life choices she made in relationships caused her to develop her reliance on substances.

It took a while for this client to get her life back on track. While she was doing so, her children lived with her family. This client's blueprint was formulated from a biological predisposition, augmented by early trauma, and was then followed by abusive relationships. She developed her addiction to cope with the feeling of not being good enough. At present, this client continues to work to repair the damages from her life choices that were dictated by the blueprint of her life.

I will now ask you some reflective questions about dependency:

Check-In Questions

What was your first experience with alcohol like? Was it when you were a teenager?

Are you concerned with your consumption of alcohol? If so, why?

Do you use alcohol or drugs to increase your feelings?
When you feel happy or sad do you use alcohol to increase these feelings?

Have you had complaints from anyone in your life about your alcohol consumption? If so, how does alcohol impact these relationships?

If you have concerns about your drinking habits, would you be able to go six weeks without alcohol? If not, why?

Have there been issues with alcohol or drugs in your family?

Case Study Four: Grief

A young female actress, aged thirty-eight, had issues relating to her marriage. She was in a great period of her life. She had everything that a woman would want: she was married to a lovely, kind, and caring man; she had two beautiful stepchildren; and she had a phenomenal extended family. Her life was ideal—or so she thought. She had worked hard on her acting career and she was getting a lot of breakthrough roles, but then she started to second-guess where she was in her life. She had her ideal career, and supposedly the perfect man, but she was unhappy.

Early Childhood

She was born into a very affluent family of entrepreneurial parents. She was an only child, which came with perks, but at times she was also lonely. My client went to prep schools, and her parents made sure they provided her with all the things they didn't have when they grew up. From quite a young age, she was involved in the arts and she participated in dancing and singing competitions. As a young girl, she was allowed the space to develop into an independent, passionate person. The space her parents had brought her into was one that allowed her to evolve into the person she was meant to be.

Teenage Years

She enjoyed all the things that teens do. She spent time with her friends and, just like any typical girl, she enjoyed shopping, hanging out with friends, and was interested in boys. She also had a good sense of what she wanted in a relationship and learned a lot about herself as she had several boyfriends. She was quite attractive and didn't have any problems attracting boys. Even though she enjoyed dating, she didn't allow relationships to take her away from other things that were equally as important. For example, she did very well in school. She focused on her studies because her parents imparted the importance of having an education, regardless of her aspirations to become an actress.

She was involved in a lot of activities, such as tennis and horse-back riding. Both of these were passions of hers, but her biggest passion was to become an actress. She spent hours and hours in her room practicing acting, dancing, and singing; her parents supported her through her practice. She was involved in voice, dance, and acting lessons with the best teachers available. Both parents provided her with the space and opportunity to improve her skills because they could financially afford it. She spent quality time with her parents and they took her on vacations to Europe for the summer.

Early Twenties

My client decided to pursue a business degree because she had been exposed to business throughout her life. Her parents were so proud of her when she graduated with honours while concurrently maintaining her passion for the arts. She went to a nearby university, which enabled her to see her parents on the weekends. Her residence was only an hour away and sometimes they went for dinner together during the week.

As she was away at school, her parents started to take the time to travel as a couple again, which they hadn't done since their daughter was born. One weekend, her parents went away and, on the way home, their private plane crashed. Both of her parents were killed instantly.

My client was twenty-two years old and orphaned. Immediately, she went into work mode. She was very well taken care of financially, so she didn't have any concerns there. However, she decided she needed to take a more secure route in life rather than acting, so she pursued an MBA. She was distraught that her parents were gone, but she quickly moved on from the grief and focused on her career. She took care of her parent's estate with such poise and charm that her extended family members were not too concerned about her. She went back to school, finished her MBA, and graduated at the top of her class. After graduating, she landed a prestigious job in the financial sector, and she quickly climbed the corporate ladder due to her ethics and hard work.

For the next couple of years, she focused on her work and achievements to the point where she became a workaholic. She had a relationship, but it wasn't serious, and then she became involved with her present husband. He was a long-time friend with whom she had started to become close. He was a gentle and very sweet man, providing her with safety and security. He was someone whom she could rely on. At first, she wasn't attracted to him in a romantic way, but eventually her feelings changed and they started dating. He charmed her to the point where her feelings for him became romantic. He was one of the nicest guys she had ever met in her life. He swept her off her feet and they got married.

Thirty-Five Plus

As her marriage progressed, life was very good. Routines were set up and the stepchildren adjusted to their new situation. At first it was difficult for the children, but as time progressed things seemed to flow. My client relished her relationships with her stepchildren, her in-laws, and all the additional family members that came with her new husband. Life was secure and safe, and she was happy. She was very content with her husband and she felt so lucky for having married her best friend.

As the years progressed, she started to pursue her acting career again, and he felt alive and passionate in a different way. She hadn't felt this way in a very long time. She had focused on business, which wasn't her passion. With acting, she finally felt connected to a part of herself she had cut off for years. However, the more she focused on acting, the less she felt connected to her business career and the life that she had built for herself.

Even though she was happy in pursuing her passion in acting again, she started to realize that there wasn't any physical intimacy in her marriage. Her husband was very supportive of her in every way, but she started to feel as though he was more of a friend rather than an intimate partner. She recognized that when her husband travelled she did miss him, but not in a way that a wife misses her husband. Upon his return home, there often wasn't any physical intimacy. She felt that something was wrong with their marriage, so her husband persuaded her to enter counselling.

This client didn't have any prior experience with the counselling process. Her idea of counselling came from what she saw on television. As the process was explained to her, my client grappled with the concept of openly sharing her feelings and she eventually opened up to the process.

My client was very confused and she felt silly that she was talking to someone about something so personal. She realized that things had to change in her life because she was hurting her partner who was madly in love with her. At the time of counselling, they hadn't had any sexual intimacy for a year. The couple recognized that they needed to do something different. Their lives were relatively stable, but their connection was blowing in the wind. My client really wanted to use counselling as a space where she could really understand herself and, in turn, understand the choices she had made in her life.

This was not an easy task. My client had never participated in deep reflective experimental work in her life. She truly cared about the man she was married to and recognized the block in their relationship was within her. My client shared a lot about her upbringing—it was clear that she was brought into a world full of love and care. She was an only child, so she was showered with an abundance of financial and emotional support. She relished the experiences her parents exposed her to and she realized with their sudden loss that she had cut off a part of herself. She didn't allow herself to grieve in a normative way.

At the time of her parents' death, she plunged into work and the other systems in her life that restored the safety and security she suddenly and severely lacked. She took on the role of being hyper-responsible. There wasn't anyone left. She felt like an orphan even though there were other people in her life. Her safety and security had been ripped away, so she filled this need as best she could with work. She then married the most safe and secure man who could bring back the stable element her parents represented.

When my client acknowledged the choice she made in her partner was based on safety and not love, this put her in a difficult position. She didn't want to lose this fantastic life that she had built, but she had to honour the people and space that she had created. She needed to make the best decision for these people in her life. After an arduous process in marital counselling, she finally realized that she needed to end her marriage.

When her parents died, the passion for life that she had as a young adult was abruptly ripped away. She worked towards restoring this passion with her acting career and she realized she didn't need a safe and secure family any longer. She wanted to feel passionate again. She wanted to experience this in the true sense of the word. Her counselling lasted over six months, but the client did eventually end her marriage. Now, she can forge on and live her life in passion, even though she experienced such significant losses so early in her life.

I will now ask you some reflective questions on grief:

Check-In Questions

Has there been a significant loss in your life that may have impacted some of the choices you have made?

What is your passion in life?

Are you fulfilling that passion to your fullest potential? If not, why?

Are you are maintaining relationships in your life because you have a fear of being alone?

If you were lying on your deathbed, would you say you lived your life with meaning and purpose?

In reflecting upon these various case studies, it becomes obvious that we may not be aware we are replicating the unconscious actions that affect us. We often start to ask ourselves these deep introspective questions, and it is when we are able to have a clear conversation with ourselves that see how we have created the lives that we presently live. For the most part, we are impacted by many variables that affect the choices we make, but it often takes a life circumstance or even a bodily cue for us to slow down and listen to what we truly value.

Chapter 10:
My Reflection on My Life

In this chapter, you will focus on an exercise that you can use to connect to some of your core values.

Exercise: Miracle Question

I would like you to find a comfortable spot to sit where there aren't any distractions. Then, engage in a relaxing pattern of breathing. Breathe in and out multiple times, only focusing on the breath coming in and out from the bottom of your nostril. When you find yourself relaxing, picture yourself on your deathbed. Imagine yourself at an older age and then reflect back on your life. Allow your thoughts and emotions to flow freely. You will send all the information to the present-day you. You will focus on all the things you have accomplished throughout your life. Let your thoughts flow as long as you need to and, when you come back to the present, write down everything about what you value.

This exercise is definitely not for the faint of heart. Your inner voice is the best road map you can ever have for your precious life journey. As you do this exercise, it is imperative that you allow yourself to flow like you are on a cloud. This will be a very telling experience because it gets you connected to living life on your own terms. I truly believe that we all have the answers to our questions within our reach, but sometimes they are tucked away beneath the conscious levels that we use day to day.

My Personal Reflections and Answers

Looking around on my last day, I would have liked to live life to the fullest. I would have liked to max out on all the richness of life instead of being afraid to forge into the areas of life that may have been laden with fear.

As I think about my life up until this point, I realize that there are a lot of aspects that I could have changed, which are glaringly obvious to me now but were not so obvious to me in the past. There are aspects of my life that I love, but there were also things like my marriage and corporate position that I kept going along with only out of fear. As I reflect back on my life and see the life that I lived, I first and foremost see the gift of the great people in my life. I have many connections to others.

The strongest connection I have with another person is with my son. He has been full of vim and vigour ever since he was born. Growing up, he has been full of integrity and I hope he will continue to live and love life like he is the ultimate human being. I hope he will exude warmth like he did the day he was born. With his piercing lovely blue eyes, he will bestow the look of gratitude and kindness that I strive to enrich in him every day.

I hope he will have a full life with a career where he uses his creativity, just as he did from the times he climbed to the sink in our kitchen to make what he called "speriments." In his future, I hope he will keep the same fascination in his work as he had in his play as a child. I hope he will enjoy the craft that he picks for his lifework and enjoys the richness of creativity, meaning, and purpose in his work, just like I enjoyed it throughout my life. I hope that he will not consider his career a job but a calling.

I hope that in his future, my son will love unconditionally and attract a like-minded person who will share his values. As I have told him, I would like to have loads of grandchildren whom I will babysit so that he can spend time with his partner. Once he is older and has his own family, I hope to have many get-togethers with him and his family and that he will love spending quality time with us all together.

I have had richness in my relationships with my mom and dad. I have enjoyed the love that I share with them and I have loved them in my own special way. I have relished the times that I have had valuable moments with them in the later stages of their lives, when we have reminisced about our lives together, the time I have enjoyed with them as a couple, and also my time with them when they were apart. I have continued to spend time in Trinidad with my dad's family and have enjoyed the legacy of his family. I have enjoyed the time his family has spent with my son and I, and we have relished the stories about my time with them as a child. They have begun to develop special relationships with my son, as only grandparents can. I want my son to experience the love from my parents that I felt I had missed as a child.

My time with my brother and sisters has been maintained as richly as possible. We have enjoyed our time together even with our differences. My son and I have also spent important time with my nieces, nephews, and my brother's and sisters' whole families. I have enjoyed watching my son as he has become part of my family. Here, he has learned many of the extended family values and I hope he will continue to learn about his Trinidadian heritage and I know that, as part of two cultures, he will always respect diversity and differences.

My friendships have continued to be rich throughout my life. I have continued to spend time with all my friends. Their children have become a part of my family and my son has become equally as close to them. My annual birthday celebration has been my greatest gift with the joy of connection with all the people who I call friends in the same room sharing drinks and food, laughing, and having a fun together every year.

In my career, I have continued to help others, either in counselling or through teaching, and I have recently embarked upon writing. I hope I have touched as many lives as possible by communicating the life lessons I have learned with others on a continual basis. I have enjoyed my career path and have continued to be the consummate learner regardless of my age or stage.

I have travelled a lot and learned about the world each and every time I travelled. I have continued to be intrigued by the richness of people and life. I have practiced being self-aware so I could continually grow as a person. I have allowed myself to see the richness of each and every moment as I continued to practice mindfulness. I have laughed every day, learned new skills often, and have sung and danced as much as possible. I would like to have played a lot more in my life. If I had, then I would have made a lot of mistakes but I would not have been so hard on myself for making them. I have tried many activities and I would like to try more.

I have now met a life mate with whom I can enjoy unconditional love. With him, I enjoy a rich, deep, caring, passionate, emotionally, and spiritually aware individual. I have risked loving again. I have learned lessons from my past failures and have pushed forward to fully trust again now and in the future. Now that I have found love again, I would like to relish the years with another human being where I can be fully myself, where I can be "real" again, and know that that person accepts me for who I am. I will also accept my life mate for who he is and we will work through our differences as they arise. I will continue to bring heightened knowledge of what I have learned from my past to the present and trudge through the rest. I will be completely present regardless of issues that arise.

I would like to continue writing more books that assist people in gaining self-awareness so that they can live their best life possible. I would like to do speaking engagements and workshops all over the world to spread my message.

In the future, I wish to return to Trinidad and start an organization that assists people who need help. I would like to give back to the environment that I grew up in because I feel like I owe a debt to the place where I came from, and that giving my wisdom back to Trinidad would mean leaving my legacy in a place that needs it. I would like to start an organization that gives scholarships to less privileged individuals who cannot afford the opportunity to study and live in a first world nation. In my organization, I would teach life skills and resiliency skills to the less fortunate in hopes that it would make a difference in their lives.

Check-In Questions

Who would be the people you would like to surround you on your deathbed in your last moments?

Are these people in your life now?
If not, who should not be there? If so, why?

Is there someone who needs to be there but isn't?

What are the qualities of the people you keep around you at your present stage of life?

What are the qualities of the people you have eliminated?

What would you have done to live your life to the fullest? Would you have done anything differently?

What activities have you done?

Are there any activities you would stop doing? If so, why?

What would you have done differently in your career?

What qualities would you like to be most remembered for?

What qualities do you want to immediately discontinue?

Is there a legacy you would like to leave to your children? If so, what is it?

Chapter 11:
Listen to Your Inner Voice

Throughout my life I didn't slow down often enough to listen to what was in my best interest. When I had my son, I had to ensure that he was going to be exposed to all the things necessary to make him the best man possible. I can truly say that having my son was a defining moment in my life. I felt this was when my reconnection process started to happen and I felt the real value of connection in life. This was also when I realized that I was not living my value, and I started to take inventory of my life. My life started to take a metamorphic shift; my inner voice grew louder. I could no longer ignore my inner voice. The things I valued became obvious to me.

I needed to demonstrate to my young child a strong sense of self, and how could I do this when I was not living this kind of life myself? I needed to start listening, and the messages were all around me—for the first time, I started to pay attention.

When I was pregnant, my ex-husband went out all night and showed up at 6:00 a.m. with a friend who he called his "human shield." I was devastated; it was New Year's Eve and I had spent it alone. I realized he did not value me as a person or as a mother to be. However, I ignored this message and plugged along. In retrospect, I ask myself, "Why?" Well, where was I going to go? I was five months pregnant at the time, but the scenario became worse. I understood that the legacy of what I was creating for my son was less than positive, but I still held out the hope that my partner would change and put his son and myself first. Finally, I could not take the denigration of my marriage any longer, and I decided to separate from my husband. It was at this point that I listened to my inner voice. Before listening to my inner voice, I endured a lot. It took so much for me to decide that I needed to end my marriage, but it was such a necessary step in my journey to heal. I had decided that living alone with my young son was well worth the sacrifice. My inner voice was there all along, even when my husband cheated on me, but I still continued to repeat the pattern that I had learned as a child.

Like my mother, I accepted the incessant apologies and promises to be better from my partner after each dispute. This cyclical pattern only made the situation more unbearable as time passed. In my separation, I can truly say that I was numb to that process.

I had finally made the big step for what was right for my son and me but, in retrospect, I question whether I actually did. I did separate physically, but I was still emotionally attached to my ex-husband. During this initial separation I felt as if I was finally valuing myself, but I was just going through the motions. I didn't build the emotional muscles that I needed to make the necessary shift to create real change.

I was still in love with my husband and, deep down inside, I hoped this time apart would help him to realize the immense pain and loss he put us through. This was not the case. My ex barely saw our son during this separation and he continued with his irresponsible ways; drinking and behaving like an adolescent child. Once again, I listened to my inner voice and I took a really big step, but I still didn't make the necessary change that was going to give me the kind of life I knew I wanted. I had left, but I sat in quiet desperation and gave up my power to another. I prayed that my ex would make changes, reclaim his position in his family, and reclaim the people he loved. I was repeating the exact same pattern as my mother. I was staying for my own needs under the pretense that this was for my son. I had given up my power by telling this man that he could do to me what he wanted and that I would sit patiently and hope that he would make the best decision for my life. This was a quality that I so despised in my mother, and I prided myself in saying that I was strong to her—but really, I was just like her in this respect.

I remember the countless times that horrible things happened in my parent's marriage. My mother tried to leave my dad many times, but she said that she could not leave us behind. Then, what was my excuse? I did not have six kids or live in a third world country. My setback was the fear of the unknown and being alone. The disrespect that my siblings and I felt towards my mother in her choice to stay was something that I pushed back into the recesses of my mind when I reconciled after a year and half of separation. Then, there was a point when I needed major surgery and, once again, I succumbed to the belief that I couldn't do things on my own and I didn't listen to my inner voice.

Next, my ex and I decided to reconcile, even though my inner voice told me this was wrong. One night, while we were in the process of reconciling, and I still had my stitches in from my major surgery, I went to look for my husband. I walked into his local watering hole to find him with a woman on what looked like a date. I lost it on him and the woman he was with; however, I reconfirmed to him that I was not valuable because I still continued with our reconciliation counselling. Now I ask myself, why would anyone value someone who they realize doesn't value herself? I reconciled with him for four more horrendous years, even though inwardly I knew our relationship would never work out. I reconciled with him mainly because of my need to get the love that I wanted from a man, but he was incapable of the emotional change necessary to repair the damage he had created.

Prior to reconciliation, my husband and I started counselling and the first order of business was to live together again. Did we have the skills? I foolishly thought we did, but really, I was not thinking this through from a logical place—only from an emotional perspective. I wanted my family back together at all odds, so I ignored anything that might destroy that—even my own doubts. The old behaviours that had caused the separation became worse, but once again I put my blinders on, ignored my inner voice, and worked hard to keep things intact. The same dynamics still existed; I wanted a family life while my partner wanted to be married with all the perks but without the trap-pings of commitment. Those four years of reconciliation were very long and arduous. The volatility got worse and so did my partner's regressive behaviour.

I kept trying to maintain a positive environment, but then my son started to see that there was a lot of drinking going on around him and we didn't do anything together as a family. My son and I only ever spent time together by ourselves while my ex stayed up until the early hours of the morning getting intoxicated and then slept late into the afternoon. My son was learning that it was okay to do these things and he thought that it was normal. I needed to pack up my self-respect—what little of it was left—and start to set the example of what I wanted my son to learn.

It took me almost ten years to value myself, but I finally real-ized that I was being selfish, so I started to listen more clearly to my inner voice. Here I was raising a young man who would see that his mother did not value herself and this was suddenly the impetus that I needed to leave my marriage.

I remember after we separated, my son, who was nine years old at the time, said to me, "Mom, where is my bedroom?"

"I don't know," I told him.

"Above the kitchen," he said.

This smart young child had heard all of our disputes that had taken place in the kitchen. All along, I had fooled myself into thinking that I was hiding my hurt and pain. In reality, I was teaching my son that he needed to disconnect from what he was feeling. I could now see that he was scared, but that he had stifled this until after the separation. I had to find a way to help him let go of this fear.

My inner voice also told me that there were certain things I needed to purge from my life. I needed to let go of the destruc-tive patterns of the past. I had seen my mother stay with my father when the relationship was over, and this was a possible reason as to why I had also stayed in a dysfunctional marriage.

I felt I was passing this family legacy of dysfunction on to my son, which my inner voice told me I should not do. When my marriage ended, my ex did not sit with my son and discuss the ending of our marriage. Instead, I had to sit with him and explain to him that his parents' marriage was over. In a regressively childish way, he left the matrimonial home when I returned from a trip and, shortly afterwards, he served me with separation papers. I didn't have anyone who could work with me to stop this generational pattern, nor anyone to tell me that what I was going through was significant. I only had my inner voice to guide me.

I also let my inner voice guide me in what kind of partner I envisioned for myself and what was normal in a relationship. For years I told myself that I needed to be more patient and understand that couples have differences all the time. What I realize now is that sometimes there are differences that aren't rectifiable. My partner and I had a great life together as teenagers and young adults, but we were not meant to share a long-term life together. This is still a harsh reality for me to admit. We always prided ourselves in saying that we were so lucky because we had something that others could only dream of. However, this was a stage-related concern. In order for our marriage to survive, I would have had to lose my voice and soul forever and live against all the beliefs that I valued.

I realized what I needed in a partner within two short years after my separation. I need a partner who was emotionally mature and understood his role in an ever-evolving relationship. I needed someone who was self-assured and had a real sense of self. Self-esteem and confidence are both key traits and, along with this, my partner would need to have a real sense of what was valuable to him. I needed someone who had the same core values as I did, especially when it came to family. Without this value, I couldn't maintain a long-term relationship; hence, the ending of my marriage when this life stage began.

I also needed a partner who could accept me for who I was. I needed someone who would stand with me through thick and thin, who could give me unconditional positive regard and, in turn, I could give the same to them. Most importantly, they needed to be very family orientated.

In the end, my inner voice told me that I wanted to impart the values of reciprocity, respect of family, and unconditional positive regard onto my son. In order to allow my son to learn these values, I needed to not only listen to my inner voice, but I also needed to value myself. If I followed this behaviour, I could create a legacy of healthy behaviour for my son and break the generational patterns from my family of origin.

Check-In Questions

How do you slow your thoughts and feelings on a routine basis?

Are there things that you do to listen to your body daily?

How do you know when things are not going right for you in your life as opposed to facing a minor annoyance?

How do you stay connected to values, beliefs, and assumptions?

Close your eyes and think of the various relationship areas of your life. Rate them based on what your body tells you: one being difficult and ten being great.

For the relationships that you rated with lower "more difficult" numbers, ask yourself what you need to make these relationships better for you. Do this daily if necessary until you can hear what your inner voice has to say.

Chapter 12:
Legacy to the Future Generations

Upon my reflection, I realize what a great opportunity it is that we have the chance to choose and work towards what we want in our lives. As human beings, we are lucky that we can formulate whatever we want and create a path to achieve our dreams. As I reflect and write, I realize that so much of what I wanted in my life was based on early experiences. As a young child, I absorbed so much from those experiences, and now I realize that, independently, I could decide what my ideal would become. My ideal blueprint was often based on what I thought would be really good in my life. Sometimes, I experienced my ideal, but more often my ideal blueprint came from snippets of what I had and what I did not have.

My main legacy thus far has been teaching the importance of taking care of the next generation so that we continue to make a better place to live. I would like to assist women because they are usually the emotional keeper of the families. I would like to help them impart their need to use their resilience to take care of the future generation. This would include teaching life skills by offering retreats where they could return to their families bringing all the richness that they need to care for them.

As I think back on my life, I wanted everything to be perfect. Why wouldn't I want perfection? Is that not our birthright? As a child, I wore rose-coloured glasses: I recognized I could have everything I wanted in my life. I became a sponge and soaked up what I wanted. In my early stages of life, with my mind acting as a video camera, I took millions of snapshots of my ideal. I looked at the people around me and decided what I loved in them and I wanted to those lovely qualities in my relationships. When I think of my parents and the love that they demonstrated to my siblings and me, I decided I would ensure that my children felt the same love. I saw how much they sacrificed for their children, so I did the same for my son.

Upon reflection, I realize that their innate ability to show love to me was not common in the world. As a young child, I didn't think it was possible that other children would actually mouth the words, "My parents never loved me." As an adult and as a psychotherapist I have unfortunately heard these words too often.

In my own relationships, I couldn't use my parents' relationship as a guide to create my ideal, but there were a lot of other adults around me who had great relationships. I talked with them a lot about their relationships and, most importantly, I noticed how they treated each other. Then, I started a checklist in my mind. I would not settle for less than having all the qualities necessary to have a successful relationship. My ideal negated a lot of things I remembered from my parents' relationship. A lot of the time, television and movies filled in the gaps where I needed more information.

I felt fortunate to have my friends' parents available for guidance and modeling as I searched for my Mr. Right. I felt so smart at such a young age. I had control of my choices as I went to find my Mr. Right. I went through a couple of immature relationships prior to meeting my husband but, in retrospect, my relationships were at a very young developmental age. I had a lot of crushes and short-term dates, and then I found my Mr. Right. But, was I too young? I didn't think so because I had found what I needed at the time.

When I married at age twenty-two, I felt I could now focus on the other normal developmental things that this stage brought. My friends thought I was nuts for settling down into marriage at such a young age, but what did they know? They hadn't found their perfect mate, so I was glad that I had the guts to go after what I wanted. When I was fifteen, I liked a guy who was a bit older than me, so I called him and we dated. From that experience, I always thought if I liked someone then I should go after them. I really didn't have to do much when I met my Mr. Right. It was simple; we fell in love. I thought that I had been successful in finding my ideal mate—and maybe he was right for me at that younger life stage.

At this young life stage, I was also confident that I had figured out all the areas of my life. I felt like I knew exactly what I needed; all I needed to do was create these blueprints in a very concerted way. I developed a plan of how things were going to look in my life and then I went out in pursuit of what I was looking for to fit into my pre-set template. I just thought I had to work hard and then I could have anything. Having a great work ethic had gotten me very far in my career, so I applied this strategy to most other areas in my life including my relationship.

When I was eleven I had figured out what I really wanted in my life. For me, my friendships came very easy. I wasn't the most popular in school, but I had a solid group of friends and I was a part of the groups I wanted to be. I never really struggled to make friends. I believe my natural ease at creating connections with other people made it easy for me to make friends and, at present, I still continue to be very comfortable in social situations.

I replicated the qualities and situations I liked that I saw in other people and their relationships, and when the areas of my life lacked appropriate role models, I searched voraciously until I found the information that I needed. I might have overlooked qualities that I later realized were very valuable. I made decisions about people and circumstances that may have been potentially plagued by the pain of my life choices. My ideals were skewed by limited amounts of information and I should have explored a lot more before making major life decisions.

I set out on our journey together with all the vim and vigour that I could muster and the image of a perfect life clear in my vision. I used a lot information gathering, but I failed to share this information to get a better perspective. I wonder whether I would have taken the time to reflect on the limitations of my

A Therapist Insider's Guide on Relationships

ideals if I had a mentor. At eleven years old, I probably would
not have listened, but I think as a teenager I would have listened
to someone who gave me guidance. In my culture there was a lot
of advice given, but there wasn't any space for reflection.

When I became a therapist, I thought this profession would
flop. I wondered who would want to seek therapy. But, that
was a different time in the world. As my career proceeded
and Hollywood glamourized therapy, everyone appeared to be
comfortable talking about seeing a therapist. Today, I know the
stigma still exists, but I think almost everyone should consider
this introspective lens into their lives.

Going back to our child-like state

As we reflect on the vast messages that we would like to pass
on to future generations, it becomes imperative that we are truly
in contact with what we value based on play. I believe when we
come into the world, we come as a blank slate with a lot of core
information that is unique to each and every one of us. I also
believe that being in contact with our child-like state is a key
part in connecting with the real essence of who we are and what
flows from us—a space that is very powerful.

Next, I would like to engage you in an exercise that will connect you with the little person of your earlier years.

Reflective Time: Float Back Technique

Find a quiet place in your home where you are able to meditate.
Get in a mediation position where you are able to have your back
straight against a wall or a chair. Then, start to find the natural flow
of your breath. With each inhale, try to push away all thoughts
or feelings that may be obstructing relaxation. Acknowledge the
thought or feeling, and then let it float away like a cloud in the
sky.

Once you're relaxed, float back in time to when you were

around five years old. Picture how tall you were. Look at your entire body. What are you wearing? What does your face look like? What are some of the things that are going through your head at five year old?

Spend some time with your little self and ask him or her for pebbles of wisdom. What did you do to have fun when you were a child? What things do you need to know about yourself that you might have lost contact with at your current age? Understand what things or activities made you happy. Take the time and collect as much information as you need and, when you are ready, come back to consciousness and open your eyes. Lastly, write a letter to your present day self about what you learned from your little self.

It is so insightful when we are able to come in contact with the part of ourselves that we have become disconnected from. This earlier child state is a time when we know a surprising amount about ourselves. But, as my personal life's events altered, how my life played out became the reality. It is important to make contact with our younger selves so we can start to enjoy that sense of play or creativity that lies right below the surface of our unconscious.

I am always amazed when I do this exercise because I'm able to visualize myself so clearly as a young child. The space that I go back to is freeing; I was such a happy child before I understood that there were concerns within my family.

As a child, I talked all the time and played for hours. When we get disconnected from that child-like state of ourselves, it's because there was something that we needed to disconnect from. When I grew older and started training to be a therapist, I realized that my child-like state was tucked far away. I love being connected to my child-like state, but due to my lack of physical and emotional safety, I locked that connection away and concentrated on controlling other avenues of my life to rid myself of the things I could not control.

In my family pictures, I wear the face of a little girl that had grown sullen and disillusioned in life. Sadly, it was during the innocence of my childhood that I started to take life seriously. In my culture, even though we had fun times, I always found myself needing to be in control. This sense of control makes sense to me now because if I didn't have it, then my life would seem even more out of control than it actually was.

In my family, we had fun as children, but the fun was often cut short because my family's issues dictated when and how often we were carefree and having fun. Now I realize that having fun was something I prescribed on my terms, but rarely was I truly in the moment. I had fun, but I definitely guarded myself internally on an ongoing basis. My role in my family, in clinical terms, was as the "parentified" child. I became the kid who protected my mother when she could not protect herself. This was a role I took on quite early and continued to hold for a lot of years, even after getting married at twenty-two. My partner didn't appear to have any of these characteristics when I first met him. I mainly thought that he was a lot of fun, but my need to have someone light-hearted showed in time when he didn't want to evolve emotionally with me.

While I reflect back on my early years of life, I realize I was robbed of precious years of my childhood because I became so focused on what my parents were going through that I didn't focus on the key things I needed to, in order to evolve and grow. I would scream at my dad when he was mean to my mother. I would get in the middle of physical fights and I didn't think for a second that I might get hurt.

When I started to get connected with my inner child state, I realized I had missed so much of my childhood. Regardless of the circumstances, I still had a lot of fun memories with my siblings, but the real me was not allowed to show until a lot later in my life. At present, when I'm able to connect with an inner space, I discover so much about myself. I realize I like being responsible, but not at the high level that I had taken on in my life. I recognize I like to take care of others, but I also relish the times when I allow others to take care of me. I'm a lot fun and I am super creative, but that isn't something I realized until lately. I used to shy away from trying new things because I was self-conscious, but now I like to challenge myself to grow as a person, so I often try new things.

A lot of activities have allowed me to get connected with my inner self, which show me who I really am. These activities allow me to be completely in the moment. One of the first activities that allowed me to connect with my inner self was scuba diving. It was one of the most challenging experiences I had ever had in my life, but as I conquered this challenge, my self-esteem grew immensely. As I trained, I realized I had a fear of being under water and losing control. I panicked several times, scrambling to the top of the pool because I felt like I was going to die; however, I kept at it. The next scary lesson was when I had to take off my mask. I told myself that I could do it, and I did, but with a lot of fear. However, once I faced the fear, I found that being under water in that serene space was so comforting, warm, and nurturing. For the first time, I truly experienced mindfulness. I got farther past my fear each and every time I dove. My desire for that peace of mind grew, and my sense of confidence also grew.

As I reflect on many of my other activities, the most valuable thing that I do routinely is my mindfulness meditation. I practice it daily, and it allows me to clear my mind each and every morning before I face the reality of my intensely packed day. I challenge you to connect with your inner self.

Even though I had an ideal blueprint, I would have liked to be cognizant of my blind spots prior to making my life choices. My ideals were based on the decision-making process that if one quality or trait is bad, then look for the opposite quality or trait. In some areas of my life, my black-and-white thought patterns served me wrong. As an adult having gone through a lot of life lessons, I realize the importance of the grey area in making decisions. However, now I question where I should have been. Should I have been more aware of my realistic blueprint?

I have given you a few more questions than usual, because I feel like this path that we have journeyed together has given you a lot to reflect upon. The legacy for our future generations warrants more questions than the previous chapters. I truly feel that spending more time reflecting on our legacy creates a genuine path that is real within everyone. Now I would like you to lay down the book and really spend some time alone with these questions that were immensely helpful for me in the space that I was able to achieve in my life.

Take the time and really answer the questions from your deep inner knowing space.

Chapter 12

Check-In Questions

What are the qualities you need in an ideal friend?

How many of your current friends have these qualities?

Are there friendships that drain you? If so, what do you gain from these friendships?

How did you decide what qualities the ideal friendship should have?

Do you think you should have different friends for different areas of your life? If so, what is your reasoning behind this?

How many of your friendships are gratifying?

Are there friendships you need to eliminate immediately?

Who was your first significant friend as a child? Are you still friends with that person? If not, what happened?

Is there an ideal number of friends that someone should have in their life? If so, please explain how many and your reasoning behind your thought process.

What are the qualities of your ideal mate?

How did you decide on the traits of your ideal mate?

Did your family relationships impact the qualities that you need in your ideal mate?

Did you make the choice of your ideal mate on a conscious or unconscious level?

Do you have memories of a couple you knew as a child whom you may have used to formulate the qualities of your ideal mate as you observed their relationship?

Does your ideal mate mirror the same qualities that your mother has?

Does your ideal mate mirror the same qualities that your father has?

What are the qualities of the ideal family?

How did you formulate the ideal family for yourself?

What things did you envision the ideal family to have?

Is your view of the ideal family based on your primary family of origin? If so, how?

Is your view of the ideal family completely different to your family of origin? If so, how?
How did you see the interaction between your family members? Was it close, enmeshed, or distant?

Did your culture impact your formulation of the ideal family? If so, how?

Was there a family that you were exposed to in your life that encompasses the qualities of the ideal family for you? If so how so?

The ideal career?

As a child, can you remember what your thoughts were about what your ideal job would be? Did these thoughts change as you became older?

Did you pick your ideal career based on your parents' careers? If so, explain why.

Did you pick your ideal career based on someone who you were exposed to in your early life? If so, explain who and why.

What things do you need in your ideal career?

Do you know anyone who has their ideal career? Explain a little about this person and how you think their ideal career impacts their overall life.

Define your ideal view of self-care. Is your ideal realistic for you? In the last week, six months, and past year, what actions have you taken towards achieving your ideal view of self-care?

Did your ideal view of self-care develop early on, or was it something that adjusted as you proceeded through different life stages?
What is your ideal view of self-development?

What actions to you do on a continual basis to achieve your ideal view of self-development?

Where did you formulate your ideal view of self-development?

What experiences in your life have impacted your ideal view of self-development?

Describe earlier events and more recent events in your life that may have impacted your ideal view?

Chapter 13:
Lessons Learned

In life, I believe that we learn many lessons. As I recall all the things I endured as a child, I realize how often I felt unloved. I loved both of my parents intensely, but I did not understand why, if they loved me so much, they continuously made decisions to hurt me on an ongoing basis. Why did my dad treat my mother so badly while he said he loved his children? It didn't make sense, especially since I felt like my mother was a part of me, so by hurting her, he was also inherently hurting me.

I felt a lot of resentment towards my dad early on in my life. He showed me that I was not important enough for him to change his behaviour. I also learned that my mom did not value herself because she stayed in such a destructive situation. Needless to say, I learned that this environment steered me in the wrong direction, which was to focus on the pain of my past instead of manoeuvring through all the important milestones as a young adult.

In the end, I took on the role of the mediator in my family. My mother did not have a voice with my father, so I was the strong one and I protected her from him in many ways. My relationship with my father was one of anger and hostility. I loved him and hated him at the same time. It was hard to see any positive qualities in him at this stage because of the pain he caused me as a child. I needed my parents to mend their relationship and make my environment better, but they let their issues get in the way of their biggest focus, which should have been to help me succeed in life. Those years were filled with pain and disconnection. I never wanted my son to endure this kind of unhealthy family environment.

I learned many lessons in life as a child, a mother, a wife, and a woman. Below are some of the major life lessons that I have learned and want to share with you. I believe that in sharing my lessons, I will give you a glimpse into the journey I took that helped me reconnect with my true inner path. I hope that reading my journey gives you an insight into the process that was so powerful for me and that it is well within your grasp.

Lesson One: Stay Connected to Yourself

More than anything, I wanted my son to learn that he needed to stay connected to himself. This life lesson is key and there are several ways I feel I have allowed my son to learn this life lesson. I look at him in amazement and it makes me think about what my childhood was really like. I didn't have that magic connection with myself as a child—or I should say, it got lost very early—but I wanted to provide the space for my son.

As a baby, my son was a gentle soul. He was easily comforted, and I think this was a result of my yoga practice throughout his pregnancy. After he was born, he asked for what he needed through his cries and I met his needs in a consistent and timely manner. He was content and I could see that he was going to evolve in the ways that he needed to in his secure environment.

When the relational dynamics changed in our family life, there were ample opportunities for my son to listen to his inner voice. Early in our separation, his father took him for a couple of days at a time and wouldn't return him to me. Of course I was beside myself by the time he returned. I hid my feelings and asked him how his time was and he said it was good.

I did not impose my traumatic days on him. Instead, I took his lead. There have been so many times when I allowed him to speak his mind; I knew this from when he told me he could hear our arguments from his bedroom. I asked him if that was scary and then I allowed him to share what he felt. I told him that sometimes adults have conflicts, like his dad and I, but we both really love him. Having these meaningful conversations allowed my son to listen to his inner voice, learn to feel normal feelings, and not ignore what his environment and body told him. I tried to offer him a space where we could talk; each time situations like this example arose.

I tried my best to combat the lie that I had kicked out his father for no reason at all. The confusion that my nine-year-old son experienced was immense. He truly believed that I had asked his dad to leave for no reason, even though he knew there was ongoing conflict. A week after I asked him to move out, my ex visited our home. He then proceeded to verbally abuse me for an hour and a half. I had a friend there with me at the time, which created a bit of a buffer for our son. Nevertheless, the experience was not pleasant.

This was an ideal scenario to talk with my son about why the marriage was over. He could see the verbal altercations and could see that I was crying. I used this as an example to explain to him why sometimes people need to leave their partners because, even though they may still care for their partner, the partner no longer has the capacity to treat them with love or respect. My son had many questions and I answered in an appropriately developmental way by sharing what he could understand at his age.

After the separation from my husband, I then believed because I didn't have a partner who cheated on me and abused me anymore, that everything would work out—but this was not the case. I held on, even after his infidelity, but in time the emotional abuse started to reoccur. I needed to be honest with myself. If I really valued myself, I needed to purge the dysfunctional elements in my life and that meant my ex—the man who had been in my life longer than my own father. I had to come to realize that my best friend and lover had sadly morphed into someone I no longer knew and could no longer love. This meant that I needed to dismantle the only life that I had known since I was eighteen years old. The safety and security that I had so cautiously crafted had to be totally reorganized as well.

I started a life away from my family and in-laws. Our relationships with all of our friends and family were not the same after our separation. It's one thing to lose the partner who isn't the same person anymore, but everything else changes. Everyone and everything related to the life that I knew, other than my home, was gone after my marriage ended. My in-laws completely disconnected from me. Suddenly it was if I was dead and I only lived a few streets away from them. I was a distant memory at best.

Twenty-five years of memories were completely wiped out. All of our events together, including Christmas and Thanksgiving, were gone. I never even received a single phone call from his family members wondering how I was. I really did lose all my ex's family and all the friends we shared. In the end, I did not miss the people who were used to us as a couple, but I did miss the significant family members and friendships that had a large part of our lives.

During this time, I feel like my son learned that people almost die when there is a divorce and I do not think it is healthy for him or anyone else to think this. I feel this purging is a reflection on my ex's family and their lack of an ability to maintain healthy connections with significant people in their lives when there are endings in other relationships.

Lesson Two: The Costs of Divorce

There was so much loss for my son that it was difficult to keep up with everything that had changed, not only for me but also for him. Most of my relationships had been altered, but the most glaring change with my ex-husband's side of the family. It was as though my son ceased to exist to them. My son needed to know that their disassociating behaviour was not his fault. He needed to know that it was just the fact that they could not deal with the divorce and, instead, they cut all ties with, even my son.

I also shared common experiences with my son that I thought

would show him that he was not alone in what he was enduring. For example, I shared with him that I had lost my family too, but this is what often happens when a marriage ends. I also explained how I was trying to maintain a connection with my ex in-laws—his grandparents, aunts, and uncles—by having conversations on various occasions and the intermittent dinner with them, but no matter how much effort I made, the connection was strained at best. Even my relationship with the one family member whom I did see regularly became increasingly distant as time went by. I also tried to maintain phone calls so the family would be updated on my son's life, but with time this faded away too. Overall, I tried to maintain a connection, trying to show my son that even in separation relationships can still exist, but unfortunately, my son and I both learned that not all people deal with situations in the same way.

I filled my son's time, hoping he would not recognize all the loss he was experiencing from his father's side of the family, until one day he told me that he missed his dad's family. When my son told me that he needed the connection, I reached out to the family to let them know that my son missed them. I needed to demonstrate to my son that reconnection is possible even when a relationship ends.

The family shared that they felt sad for the disconnection, but that it was a confusing time for them as well. They invited my son to an event at their home and I mustered all the courage I had and I attended the family event with my son. He really enjoyed spending time with his family. I could see the calm that came over him when everyone extended love to him. I did not intend on staying for very long, but my son asked if we could stay longer, so I obliged. My discomfort paled in comparison to what I could see my son gaining from this experience. He was reassured that his father's side of the family still loved him even though they had not seen him for a long time.

The lesson learned by my son was harsh, but this also made him more connected with the people who have stayed in his life through this difficult time. Furthermore, each and every time when I purged something or someone from my old life, I could feel rebirth within myself. On the whole, I felt that I had regained my inner sense of self by doing this.

Nevertheless, the losses I experienced through the separation were immense and I understand why others who have also separated say that loss of significant relationships is often the most difficult consequence of a relationship's ending. I feel that in purging the severed connections, I could appreciate all the fantastic things that I still have in my life. The people who are in my life truly value what I am and they continually reciprocate my attention. Now my inner voice is loud enough, and on a daily basis I listen to it and make sure that I take the right steps.

Lesson Three: Maintaining a Connection to Others

As the process of reconnection took place within me, it was an ideal opportunity to share the process with my son. He started to realize that the people who came over to visit weren't his father's friends—they were mine. He asked if his father's friends didn't like us anymore. This was the opportune time to discuss with him the qualities and values in relationships.

I shared with him that a lot of these people were acquaintances and they were superficial friends because real friends would still be connected to him and to myself. It was difficult for him to understand how these people chose to no longer be our friends. He could not understand how there used to be so many people at our home but now we never saw them. I told him that real friends were there whenever we needed them, and that people who were no longer in our lives were only acquaintances and that they didn't have a deep quality of connection to him or me. He often asked why I wasn't friends with these acquaintances anymore. I told him that they decided that keeping a connection with me after my divorce was not valuable to them. There were also a lot of joint friends who we no longer connected with, and at times my son wondered if he would reconnect with them one day. I told him that in time we might see those family members and friends again if they thought it was important to reconnect with us.

During this time of losing many connections, I realized the significance of true connection with friends and family. I have always been fortunate in that I have close connections to both my family and my lifelong friends. An authentic connection is key in my relationships. I have been very connected to my friends who are authentic and have similar values as myself. I immersed myself in my connection with others and I hoped that through these environments my son would see and experience what I valued, and do the same in his life.

To help my son stay connected, I ensured that he was surrounded by my family, who showered him with loads of affection when he was going through so much loss of family. I also tried to make him understand that family is about love and connection through thick and thin. He saw that my family bonds were still strong regardless of ages or stages within the family. He experienced the quality time we had in their presence. We often spent weeks at a time with my family; we shared our space cooking, talking, and just enjoying the moment with each other.

My son often said to me, "Mom, I need to see my family—it has been a month."

This is a gentle nudge to remind me that I needed to reconnect with my family who lived nearby.

My culture is something that I also tried to connect my son to and prior to my divorce I took him home so he could experience some of the environment that made me the kind of person that I am today. My culture is about extended families; visiting and sitting around in each other's homes is something that I took for granted when I was a child, but as an adult I relish the value it brings into my life. Needless to say, my son thoroughly enjoyed my home life and I think I was able to expose him to the cultural side of my family's connection, which I had walked away from for so many years. I realized the significance of my own need for this cultural reconnection when I separated the first time in my marriage. Even though I have vowed to stay connected to my ex's family for my son's sake, my son should also maintain his connection to the island—a real part of the values of his life.

Lesson Four: The Value of Friendships

The other lesson I inadvertently exposed my son to is the element of true, deep, real friendships. My role as connector served me well over the years. I have significant friendships that I have maintained from childhood, even though we currently live all around the globe. As a young girl I realized the value of having supportive, caring people in my life. This has been very instrumental in helping me to recover from the pain of the past ten years. I consider my friends to be the family I have picked to be in my life.

As a teenager, it was difficult to start a new life in a new country and in a new community. I remember the loss I felt at first with of all my friends scattered all over the world, but with time I started to develop new connections. My friends started with one special friend who I met at the gym twenty-two years ago and now include a particular friend in each and every work environment that I have had over the years. My friendships were always dear to me, but the significance of their connection was heightened when every one of them reached out to my son and me during such a tough time. We found out who our true friends were.

The get-togethers, bonfires, phone calls, and help with things I couldn't do became examples for my son that people who really cared for us would not vanish in times of despair; in fact, they are ever more present and do whatever it takes to help us through difficult times.

I remember my son saying to me, "Mommy how many best friends do you have?"

I told him, "Too many to count."

The lesson for him was invaluable and I can see that he chooses friendships with like-minded people. Just like me, I see he has a variety of relationships and the common denominator is the realness of people, which is invaluable to me. I have friends whose acts of kindness humble me; for example, they will take me across the globe to spend Christmas with their family because of horrible issues around custody and access. In the end, the value I want to pass on is that we can all go through a tough time in life, but the blows are a lot less jarring when you have friends who care.

Lesson Five: You Need to Take Care of Yourself

I have learned in life that taking care of ourselves is not selfish. My journey has been a phenomenal one, but the biggest lesson I have learned and need to pass on is the need to take care of oneself. I took care of myself for the most part, but sometimes I did not. This is a lesson that I especially need to pass on to my son—that looking after ourselves is vital for optimal health and happiness. Inevitably, if we do not look after ourselves, then we cannot look after others.

We often talk about being healthy, but sometimes we do not follow through. I decided to become a psychotherapist because I thought I could then help others to find their path to happiness. It is quite apparent that in most areas of my life I learned to listen to what I needed to be healthy and happy. I have led a relatively healthy life, but I was repeating my family's generational pattern of putting my needs aside to keep a relationship.

I saw my mother and other female family members put up with so much to keep their families together, disregarding their own emotional and physical well-being—that's engrained in my culture. Those women didn't think of the impact that it would have on themselves and on future generations.

An example of this cultural pattern is my mother, who stayed in a bad marriage that eventually ended; she sacrificed her life for her six children and never moved on with her life. I wanted to ensure that my son saw that I cared for his father, but our relationship was unhealthy. I wanted my son to see that I left the marriage so we could have a better life. I didn't want my son to disrespect me as I did my mother. I wanted him to see that I lived my life with integrity. Regardless of what happens in my future, I left an abusive relationship because I did not want my son to witness disrespect and believe that this was normal for relationships.

My son started to see the disrespect his father treated us with in the last four years of my marriage and how unhealthy this was for the well-being of both his emotional self and mine. Each time I went back to my husband, he demonstrated to my son that being treated badly was normal for relationships. I left my husband so my son would learn that when someone treats you badly, then that person needs to take responsibility for their actions and make the change—and if they don't make the change, then it is necessary to end the relationship.

Since the end of my relationship, I have used numerous situations to explain to my son why I ended it. One of these situations was when my ex and his new partner sent the police to my home, stating I had made accusatory statements to his new partner. This was devastating for my son to witness.

My son could see my tears, and he said, "Mom, who can help us with this situation?"

"A lawyer can," I told him.

My nine-year-old son was exposed to the police and also witnessed his father's false allegations against me. This was a time when I really had to take care of myself and it was vitally important for my son see this. This was a difficult time for him, too, and what he needed most of all was comfort, which he did not receive from his father. But, I spent time with close friends and family as I waded through the aftermath of this horrendous chaos, so at least we had their support.

This one moment amongst many others that were horrendous;

nevertheless, they were invaluable teachable moments. He started to see and understand why I left this dysfunctional marriage. I broke the pattern of not caring for myself and, in turn, I have taught a little boy that his mother should be respected based on her actions. This is an adjustment that my mother, my aunts, and a lot of women struggle with as they stay in unhappy marriages to keep their families intact.

Lesson Six: Life Must Go on No Matter What

Learning that life must go on has been key in my process of healing. This is a lesson that I have also used in teaching my son that life can be tough, but we all have the ability to get through these tough times. Since my separation from my husband, there have been unhealthy situations that my son experienced during the last stages of the marriage, but the alternative of staying in a disrespectful marriage would have been much worse.

Through my actions, I demonstrated that we needed to dig deep to access our resources to get through these tough times. For us, these resources included a lot of get-togethers with my friends and their kids. At times, when I thought I could barely keep my eyes open, I forced myself to keep everything as normal and stable as possible for my son. I held elaborate birthday parties for my son and myself with a whole lot of fun and laughter. Today when I look at the photographs from these times I wonder how I was able to do this. I also planned seasonal trips to Florida with my family to ensure that I maintained as much consistency as possible. There were times when I was so emotionally drained that I would go to my family's home to rest while they cared for my son.

When I left my marriage, I did it in an inopportune time—I had lost my job—but I could not handle the stress of my marriage any more. So, there I was, out of a job and alone—this was when I dug deep. This was stress that I didn't want my son to feel, so I kept the stress to myself and I sought after the appropriate help that I needed.

I started teaching college, consulting with a psychiatrist, and eventually practicing psychotherapy again. I focused on the aspects of my life that I could control, and working had a great therapeutic element for me. Unlike my mother, who was in a completely different circumstance, I broke the cycle of trying to find the perfect time to leave my marriage. At times I wonder, "What was I thinking?" However, I realize that there isn't a right time to end a bad situation. It is more about finding the guts to acknowledge that it is going to be tough, but that staying would be worse.

I hope that my son recognizes that it takes courage to make change and it is often very difficult to do so. However, listening to what is important in life is key, and sometimes we make decisions that may have been appropriate at one stage in our lives don't suit our lives later on; this is when we have to be strong and make the necessary changes. Conclusively, we must continue to listen to the messages that life gives us on an ongoing basis.

Lesson Seven: Learning to Listen to Your Needs

I would like my son to learn that he should take his time and listen to what is important to him in life. I hope he learns to listen to his feelings as his sense of self develops regardless of the fact that he endured some turmoil during my pregnancy.

Generationally, the legacy from my family's pattern of behaviour in relationships was to learn to cut off what they feel so that they could cope with areas of their life that make them unhappy. Unfortunately, cutting off feelings comes with a lot of negative consequences. For example, people who follow this behavioural pattern will not get their needs met, they will experience inability to attract intimacy in their relationships, and they will disconnect from emotional ties due to grief.

Through my actions, my son can learn that it is possible for people to make changes. Regardless of the fact that it took me ten years to make changes, I did in fact succeed and listen to what was healthy for him and myself. My core issue of abandon-ment doesn't have to be a legacy that he carries onto the next generation. As he progresses throughout his various life stages, he should be able to make his way past all the various milestones necessary in order to listen to his feelings and validate his needs in all the relationships that he will encounter in his life.

Lesson Eight: A Sense of Self and Intimacy in Relationships

Developing who and what we are about is key for all human beings. With my limited knowledge, I embarked on my journey but, in the process, I made some decisions that were less than perfect. For the most part, I was able to figure out who I was and what I needed in my life at a young age. Unfortunately, my primary caregivers did not meet those needs.

When I was younger, I ignored the good guys and instead I enjoyed the thrill and chase of taming the men that did not want to be tamed. I thought I wanted someone who challenged me and not someone that complied with my every need. As I have grown older, I now recognize that I had the ability earlier in my life to have a great long-term relationship, but I had to get past what I thought was chemistry and passion.

I attracted very good intimate relationships in my life, but I made choices that fit my primary intimate relationship at home. I got mixed up being reminded of my primary relationship, which put me into a hyper-aroused state—and I equated this with love. When I look back, this hyper-aroused state was actually not a desirable state; however, I hoped these men would provide me with safety, security, and consistency. I realized this as I started to really think about healthy relationships.

Today, I have found these qualities in someone special, and I hope that with time, my son will be able to witness what it looks like to care for someone and treat them with love, dignity, and respect. I hope that, as my son sees me in a positive relationship with my new partner, and sees other couples and families with great relationships, it will create the necessary template for him to really think on a deep level about what he needs to be happy and have a healthy relationship.

Previously, this relationship model was missing in my life, and I feel that if had I been exposed to these qualities, then I might have slowed down long enough to recognize that the chemistry and passion that I was feeling might have been unhealthy.

Lesson Nine: The Effect that My Lessons have had on the Blueprint of My Life

As I reflect on the lessons I leave for my son, I need to ensure that he is aware of what stood in the way of the blueprint of my life. I have clearly stated that I have created an awesome life for myself. Regardless of the trips and bumps and immense pain that I have experienced along the way, it has been full of joy. I have had a lot of fun along the way.

There I was, the little girl from the islands with huge dreams and I set out to make them my reality. Now, here I am in the middle of my life, and I realize that every choice I made, whether conscious or unconscious, was in fact my own choice to make. In reviewing my assessment, most areas of my early life appeared to go through constructive and positive phases, except for my family life.

Overall, even though my intimate relationships suffered from my unmet needs, the other parts of my life were ones that I feel proud of: I have created a great career, fantastic friendships, close-knit family relationships, and I have also just recently started on the path of healthy, loving, intimate relationships. My blueprint wasn't necessarily a path that I had to take, but it was the one that I decided to take due to my circumstances. In many areas of my life, I had the skills necessary to conquer the terrain to create success, but I hit a huge pothole in the arena of healthy intimate relationships.

My blueprint dictated the journey of discovery that I took to rectify my intimate relationships so that I could continue to live a fulfilling life. I felt I did not have the necessary skills to deal with my relationships until my life erupted in my face. These skills included friendship skills, family connection skills, career development skills, and intimate relationship skills. Since I have experienced and worked towards rectification of these skills, I can now examine what skills I already had, and which ones I needed to develop.

I hope this following evaluation of my own skills will lead you to examine your own skills and help you think about which one(s) you need to work on.

1. Friendship Skills

I engaged in friendships from a very young age. I took the time to give to others and really listen to what my friends needed. I had different kinds of friendships to fulfill my varying needs. I was generally well liked, and I had figured out these types of relationships early in my life. I still have friendships from when I was three years old and I continue to start and maintain deep bonds with a lot of women in my life.

Intimacy in relationships comes quite naturally to me. In friendships, a deep love is shared between friends, but it is different from the depth of sharing with an intimate partner. The intimacy you share with your partner is on a completely different level that the intimacy of friendship. Good friendships are able to endure differences and even create changes to keep the friendships mutually satisfying. Through the years, there have been friendships that I needed to purge, but these were never significant losses in my life. I would rate my true friendships as very good.

2. Family Connection Skills

This is the area of my life that could probably fit into all three categories: the good, the bad, and the ugly. Early in my life, I struggled through a significant amount of conflict, so this stage constitutes falls into the "ugly" category. My teenage years fit into the "bad" category, and my current life stage it is the "good" category. For the most part, I have kept deep bonds with the family members who have wanted healthy relationships with me.

I have purged the relationships that haven't been healthy in my life. The level of intimacy needed for family relationships is quite deep and, as an adult, I have developed the skills to know what I need from my family. Generally, my relationships with my family are great, and I feel like I have worked hard to maintain the close positive relationships that I have.

3. Career Development Skills

This is one area of my life that I did not struggle much with, and I believed it was dependent on my input. I had a real sense of what I wanted to achieve in my career, and I set out to achieve it. I would categorize this area as "good." I have worked hard in this area of my life, but I think that comes really easy when I love what I do. I followed the path of psychology and it led me from career to career, and each step has been even more gratifying than the last. I feel privileged that I was able to figure this out at a young age.

Even when I was eleven years old, I offered support to my friends during lunchtime. This wasn't stressful—it was my calling—and I feel blessed to be able to do something that may bring people closer to living the best life possible.

4. Intimate Relationship Skills

This area of my life was definitely "ugly." However, now that I have dissected my blueprint, the ugliness is so obvious that I hope the lessons from my life situation will inspire others to look at their lives through an objective lens. I hope everyone can take an introspective look into their lives because this will allow them to be real about where things are at in their lives.

If someone is in a gratifying relationship, then they can use their knowledge to enrich the legacy they leave for their loved ones, but if not, then they can learn by taking a deeper look into their lives. The greatest value is that it is never too late to create the lives that we want, and we all have a duty to teach our children from our lessons so they can have even better lives than we had.

Are you living your best life possible? This is often a difficult question to answer, but give it some thought. Besides examining the skills we both currently have and need to develop, it is important to take the time to really get a sense of what we want in our lives. We are often so busy with our day-to-day lives that we lose contact with what we really want. For the most part, I really enjoyed the life I created, and the career I developed for myself allowed me to escape from the things that weren't working in my life.

Check-In Questions

What are some of the things that you have learned from your life that you want to pass on to your future generations?

Are there words of wisdom that you live by? If so, reflect on why these words are so important to you.

Outline some of the life lessons that you would like to pass onto your children.

Are there pitfalls in life that you hope that your children will not replicate? If so, what are they?

How can you help your children understand why they occurred in your life?

List some self-care strategies that are essential for your future family generations to incorporate in their lives.

Chapter 14:
The Blueprint of Your Life

Now comes the point where you examine your own blueprint of life. As explained back in Chapter 2, life is about choices. It is these choices that lead us to make decisions: the good, the bad, and the ugly. Ultimately, our choices reflect and create the blueprint of our life.

Good: These are choices in your life that are in line with what you value, your beliefs, and your assumptions.

Bad: These are choices that may potentially still fit in your life but they are not totally in line with your values, your beliefs, or your assumptions.

Ugly: These are choices that are totally out of alignment with your values, your beliefs, and your assumptions.

I will now discuss each of these categories in further detail and provide check-in questions and exercises after each section.

The Good

I often think that we don't stop long enough to reflect on the good things in our life. I truly believe there is so much to breathe in and be grateful for in the areas of our lives that are working well. This is when we are living within our values, and when we capture the true essence of who we are really meant to be.

While looking at the good areas of my life, the one that makes me feel more connected to a higher level of consciousness is quality time with my son. During these times, I am truly in the moment. I do not think of the millions of things that are constantly on my mind. I stop and completely take part in the experience of the present moment; this is not unlike what babies do so naturally. At a sensory level, we take in every sight, sound, taste, touch, and smell—similar to being in a meditative trance where we completely immerse ourselves in the moment.

When my son was young, we spent time playing together every day. In my house, I have a sunken living room; for months on end he couldn't get up the one step so I tried to help him manage it, but each time he rolled over and cried. Then, one day, I put his favourite toy at the top of the step. He tried excitedly that day and he made it! This was one of those memorable moments that I will carry in my mind and heart for the rest of my life. I was completely in the moment and so was he; time could have stopped and we never would have known. This is an example of the moments that I think we often do not stop to reflect upon.

Check-In Questions and Exercises

What are your thoughts when you are relishing positive moments? When you are in these moments, scan your body and get a sense of all the things that you notice.

What are your feelings? Itemize your feelings and work on remembering those feelings in your body so you can access them when you need them.

What is the overall expression of your body when you are in your positive moments? Think about your physical aspects like posture and facial expression.

Itemize all the values that you are living and practicing when you are in your positive moments.

How do your senses get altered during your positive moments? Think about sights, sounds, tastes, touches, and smells.

If others described you while you are experiencing positive moments, what descriptors would they use to describe you?

The Bad

We need to think about what aspects of our lives need to change in order for us to be happier. It is sometimes difficult to pinpoint these aspects when there are some grey areas of concern. The ugly can often be seen easily because they are what need to be eliminated immediately, but the grey or bad areas are more difficult to specify. The bad areas are the in-between things, and they can often be the most baffling, because they are neither entirely bad nor good.

Check-In Questions and Exercises

Rate these area(s) of your life with one being not so bad and ten being really bad. Where do these area(s) fit on the scale?

What are the qualities that are most disturbing in these areas?

Are they qualities or concerns where changes can be made? If so, what steps do you need to take in order to make these changes?

Create a values list for each of these areas and also create a non-negotiable values list. In each area, write down the aspects that aren't working, and whether they are negotiable or non-negotiable values.

Pretend that you went to bed and when you woke up, a miracle had happened. In the areas that you have already listed, itemize all the things where a miracle needs to happen in order for you to be happy.

Think about the ways you are dealing with these areas. Are they completely based on your choices? Or, are they impacted by someone else's choices that have been imposed on you?

Does your family impact the decisions that you make in these areas of your life?

Who would benefit the most from you making changes in these areas of your life? Who would benefit the least?

How often do you think about these areas of your life? Are the thoughts negative or positive? Itemize your thoughts on a daily basis.

What advice have your supportive, healthy friends given you about these areas of your life?

If you had one day to live and one decision left to make, what decision would you make about these areas of your life?

The Ugly

Now is the time to start down a path of self-discovery. If there is least one area of our lives that fits under the ugly category, then why are we keeping this person or situation in our lives? What is it that we are afraid will happen if we confront this situation? In my ugly marriage, I ignored messages for years to the point where our relationship as co-parents was completely unsalvageable.

We need to think about whether we have the skills necessary to make these changes in our lives. If we don't have the skills we need, then is there someone who can help us? When an area of our lives is ugly, it takes a lot of courage to face our fears—but if we don't face these fears, then sometimes the decisions get made for us.

Check-In Questions and Exercises

Meditate daily on the ugly situation. How would your life be better if this concern was taken care of? Repeat your answer to this question as a daily meditation for thirty days.

Journaling is a key element to getting in contact with the unconscious parts of our minds. Keep a daily journal and periodically reflect on entries once per week.

Discuss the ugly situation with a healthy, supportive friend for some constructive discussion of the issue.

Make a list of pros and cons to dealing with this situation.

As an experiment, flip a coin every day. If you get heads, act as if you have rectified the situation. If you get tails, act as if you are going to stay in the situation. Track your reactions to the coin toss and reflect on the experience daily.

Make a list of qualities that you value that are related to this area of your life. On the alternate side, check off how many of your life values are in this area and how many are not.

Sit in a quiet, comfortable place with no distractions and answer this question: If you were sitting on your deathbed, what words of wisdom and advice would you give to your younger self about this ugly issue?

Make a list of all the losses that you will experience if you make a decision or a change in this area of your life. Think about the people and places associated with it.

Find a quiet place and relax your body. Go back in time to your younger self. Take a look at your face, the way you are dressed.

When you are ready, ask your younger self his or her thoughts on this ugly situation. Listen to all those words of wisdom, and when you open your eyes, let your younger self guide you in writing a message to your present day self about those thoughts on the situation.

If this ugly situation stays the same, what will your life be like in one year, five years, or twenty years from now?

Life is truly an amazing process. We have the ability to alter our lives each and every day. My life lessons have been a privilege to me—the adversity and all. I would maybe alter some of the unnecessary pain that I endured, but overall, I wouldn't change much of my life.

The fabric of who I am today is based on all the things that I have experienced. My life journey has been fun, painful, joyous, and gut wrenching, but it has been my life. My blueprint led me to a space where I could gain this introspection, but perhaps it was not necessary for me to have to endure all this pain in order to gain all the positives in my life. I cannot go back and relive these parts of my life in a less painful way, but I can share the wisdom from my path with you and my future family.

Just like history, we cannot truly know who we are until we look at our past. My legacy began a long time ago, and it is my duty to carry forward the positives while making sure that the negatives are discontinued. As a young girl, I often remember thinking about all the things I wanted in my life. I wondered whether they were possible to achieve or if they were just a dream. All the years of self-doubt and all the negations that I got from others didn't help me live the best life.

I wish that I had started to listen to my inner voice long before I actually did. Perhaps I needed to set up the building blocks so that I could endure all the things that I have experienced in the last couple of years and deal with them properly. Having this phenomenal life has been a work in progress for a very long time.

On the whole, I like the life I have created over my life stages, but the one area that eventually became the area that needed the most attention was that of my emotional and intimate relationships. I have conquered a lot in other areas of my life, but this was the ugly category that always appeared to trip me up. Eventually, I was able to turn it around and acknowledge my needs in this area.

My trauma lens from a young age created a blindside that made me think I was on the right path to correcting my attachment issues. But with time, I realized I needed to stop following this path. Would I change anything in my life? I don't think I would, except for saving myself some of the heartache that I endured.

When I honoured my inner voice, I really stopped to listen to my values. I always knew what I wanted but sometimes I needed some assistance in getting there. Now, I feel I'm living my best life possible. I'm living life on my own terms, in each and every area of my life, and I feel privileged to have all the phenomenal people I have in my life. I also have a gratifying career, a great relationship with my son, I'm learning about myself in romantic relationships, and I also have the greatest family relationships and friendships.

I have finally stepped into a great chapter of my life and have taken hold of my Blueprints of Life. I hope that after reading this book, you can understand and appreciate your life journey a little more, and perhaps you'll realize that you may have defined your life path on an unconscious level. If your path has been true to you, then embrace it for what it is. If your path has led you away from a peaceful alignment of your values, then I hope my journey and reflections assist you to get back on your right path. Alter your blueprint in accordance with your life values so that you can enjoy this amazing gift we have been given, which is a great life.

Final Wrap-Up Check-In Questions

What is the biggest lesson that you have learned about yourself as you read this book?

What is the one thing that you are going to implement in the next twenty-four hours?

What ritual will you develop daily that will ensure you stay connected to your inner voice?

What is one of the most shocking patterns of behaviour in your relationships that is no longer functional?

Take thirty minutes and write out your blueprints story. Date this document. Make this into a routine exercise that you do at least once or twice per year.

Author Biography

Roxanne Derhodge always had a gift for connecting with others. She decided early in life that she wanted to make a difference in peoples' lives. In her early twenties she began working with the Metro Toronto Police assisting victims of crime. She eventually went on to head an Addictions Unit with the Niagara Health System before entering the corporate consulting field where she was responsible for over 40 companies.

During her time working as a therapist, she has devoted her training and practice to specializing in the following areas: addictions; eating disorders and body image concerns; gambling; the traumatic impact of sexual and domestic violence; managing anxiety/depression; and separation/divorce. Experienced in working with adults and children, she employs a wide variety of treatment approaches (i.e. EMDR, cognitive behavioural and narrative therapies), determined by each individual's life context.

Roxanne has a unique way of bringing her warmth and uncanny ability to read people to a platform where she is able to deliver what is needed in her work. She is an engaging presenter who makes her audience think on a deeper level about life and living it to the fullest.

About Roxanne

Roxanne Derhodge is a dynamic public speaker who has led multimedia keynote presentations and workshops for conferences, businesses, schools and other groups. As a speaker, she includes inspiring stories from her many years of practice and experience in the corporate world and the field of health and wellness consulting.

To learn more about Roxanne Derhodge visit:
RoxanneDerhodge.com

Roxanne Derhodge's other books:
Defyeneurs and *Young Defyeneurs*

Derhodge has been working in the field of psychology since 1988. She has worked with individuals, families, couples, and other groups. She worked as a health and wellness consultant for over 12 years, during which she enacted health and wellness strategies to make workplaces healthier. Her unique blend of warmth, along with her uncanny ability to connect with and decipher the needs of her clients, has made her invaluable in her field.

If you want to get on the path to be a published author by
Influence Publishing please go to
www.InfluencePublishing.com

Inspiring books that influence change

More information on our other titles and how to submit your
own proposal can be found at
www.InfluencePublishing.com

CPSIA information can be obtained at www.ICGtesting.com
Printed in the USA
LVOW05s1151031014

407019LV00006B/20/P